Please return

Animal Nature

A Portrait of Burgess Bauder

ANIMAL NATURE

A Portrait of
Burgess Bauder

by John Straley

with photographs by Ellen Frankenstein

PUBLISHED BY J. STRALEY INVESTIGATIONS
SITKA, ALASKA

Published by J. Straley Investigations
Box 273, Sitka, Alaska 99835

Library of Congress Control Number: 2018904347
ISBN: 978-0-692-09476-1

Cover painting by Steve Lawrie
Back cover photograph by Ellen Frankenstein

Printed in Canada

Book Design

CAROLYN SERVID
SITKA WILLOW CONSULTING | EDITING | DESIGN
SITKAWILLOW.ORG

Barry Burger and Burgess Bauder

 PART ONE
I Just Love the Guy

In my entire life, I have learned only three things with any degree of certainty. 1) Nothing good ever comes from using methamphetamine; 2) A black Labrador at a certain time in its life must have a ball to chase; and 3) A person should never talk with a dying man about a last request if that person isn't prepared to do what the dying man asks.

I learned this third truth when a hospice nurse called and asked me to meet Barry Burger. She explained that Barry was dying of a brain tumor and he wanted me to write a book about a local veterinarian named Burgess Bauder.

"But I don't want to write a book about Burgess," the words just came out of my mouth. "He knows I'm a crime writer, doesn't he?" At that time, I had published nine novels and a book of poetry, some articles and a few reviews. To make ends meet, I was working as an investigator for the Public Defender Agency, and I really didn't want to write a book about Burgess Bauder. For one, it was not going to pay. The problem with writing a book for someone as a dying wish is that there is no guarantee it's going to be a good book—or of interest to anyone else. There is no guarantee anyone is going to publish it, and there are very few people around who can really pay someone what it costs by the hour to write a book just for the heck of it. This is the hard economic truth of things. Which, I know, makes me the bearer of bad news to a dying man, but there you go. I just didn't want to do it.

The other hard thing is Burgess Bauder is a "character," and everyone thinks "characters" are easy to write about, but I don't think that's true.

Characters are easy to listen to and observe, they are fun to have a drink with, but often they are hard to break through to and really get to know.

I moved to Sitka, Alaska in 1977, and had known Burgess since that time. I played guitar in a band called "Three-Legged Dog"—named this after Burgess's early practice of saving dogs' lives by cutting a leg off rather than putting the dog to sleep because he didn't have the facilities to do more difficult surgery. Burgess was not happy with the band name.

I had also worked for Burgess's lawyer when some angry people in a nearby town went after his license; they didn't like the fact that Burgess used to take the testicles he had just cut from the family dog and feed them to his owl. He kept his license, but somewhat resented my middle of the road attitude toward his detractors, which did not replicate his own feelings—his more closely resembled William Tecumseh Sherman's attitude towards the confederacy on his march to the sea. Burgess was a "Character" writ large, and trying to write about him spelled trouble. I was a fiction writer, and I told this to the hospice nurse. I was not her man. There were plenty of other good writers and good people who would love this job.

Also, Barry Burger was beloved in our town. His friends had gathered around him in his final days to feed him and care for him. I did not know him well, but I knew that he was honest and paid attention to detail. He was loved intensely by his friends, and his friends were tough, hard-working Alaskans who would likewise hold me to their high standards.

Still, the nurse gave me the address where Barry was living and where friends and the other shift nurse were caring for him. And because I'm curious by nature, I asked her more questions about Barry, a man who would want a stranger to write a book about a friend rather than about himself as his dying wish.

Barry had been a carpenter and a jack-of-all-trades. He most recently had lived remotely on Biorka Island some ten miles from our town of Sitka, Alaska. He was the caretaker of a facility that was used for a wilderness alcohol treatment program for youth at risk. "Hoods in the Woods," some people called it. I knew from my own experience that there were a group of houses on a cobbled stone-and-sand beach, with a generator shack and a house for the caretaker down the cove, which had a pier and a deep-water landing. Apparently, Barry was well suited for the circumstances. He liked being alone most of the time; the program ran only part of the year and only part of the time at that. The other section of the island was used by the Federal Aviation Administration to host a major navigation beacon on Biorka for all the trans-Pacific flights going over the pole or to Asia. It was a secure facility, and for that reason there was not supposed to be any hunting on the island.

Now Barry Burger was living the last few weeks of his life in town. He had no current wife or girlfriend, but he had friends who came by to visit. He was staying in a rental cabin that had years ago been the woodworking shop of an old friend of mine. Now it was converted into a nice short-term rental. There was a bedroom and a warm stove. There was a TV but it was muted because no one wanted to listen to the election news.

Barry had been diagnosed with a malignant brain tumor only weeks before. He was not pursuing any curative treatment in Sitka, and it was my understanding he was not going to pursue any experimental or alternative therapy anywhere else. His condition was dire and he was calm about it. He wanted to leave a legacy about his appreciation for his friend Burgess Bauder, the veterinarian, and he wanted to see me about the book I was going to write about Burgess.

The nurse gave me the directions to Barry's little house in town one more time, and this time, I wrote them down. I don't remember telling her that I would be there at a certain time and date, but I must have because when I hung up, I had a heavy weight in my heart, as if I were already haunted by the commitment, selfish pig that I am.

Decisions are hard for me to make. I am more prone to take "Smoke's Way." I slither out of or toward containment, under cracks in the door or between the panes of glass. I worry that sometimes I let myself get pushed around, and then I well up with resentment. I was a horseshoer when my wife moved to Sitka, and for all the bears and deer on Baranof Island, there were no horses. Sitka turned out to be my natural home, part urban, part wild, but I never would have chosen it myself. Neither would I have chosen to become an investigator. I didn't really want to be a Private Investigator—it was a pity job, but nonetheless, the perfect job for me that a friend gave me when I lost a job working in the woods. Things had seemed to turn out fine for my wife and me, but it wasn't until we had a baby in our thirties that we both really started making decisions. I'm the kind of person who tends to see both sides of every situation…almost to the point of standstill. It's not a surprise to me that I ended up as a criminal defense expert. Doubt was the gold I mined.

I didn't know it then, but when I had hung up the phone I had already made a decision to write a book, because there wasn't going to be any saying "no" to Barry Burger, and somehow that sense was setting up like mortar in my chest as I drove down the road to his rental house in town on the night they were making pizza and I was designated to talk with him about the book.

The doorbell rang and another nurse, who was a cheerful young man, met me and took me in where a party of friends were eating pizza and laughing. Barry was in a wheelchair, smiling, grateful for all the good company. He extended his hand, and started right in on me.

Barry wasn't having any of my excuses. He sat me down and swatted each of them away like black flies. Burgess would cooperate with me, he said. The book could be as long or as short as I wanted. There was no deadline by which it had to be completed. ("Heck, I'm not going to read it.") If it never gets published, that's fine. ("Just have a few printed so some folks around town can read it and you can own the story if you can sell it later on.") He had already asked Ellen Frankenstein to be the photographer, a woman I knew and a woman Burgess was comfortable with—Burgess had officiated at her wedding when she married a diving buddy of his. She would have access to Burgess and would get terrific shots. I knew a printer, a good book designer, and a great editor who I had to work with because my mechanical skills are a bit rough because of my dyslexia. Barry showed no concern. He had money to pay for their costs.

"Why?" I asked him. "Why a book about Burgess?"

"I just love the guy," he said, and then he told me why.

Barry Burger and Burgess Bauder initially became friends because of people's good-hearted stupidity when it came to the local deer.

First, some geography: Baranof Island is easily found on any map of southeastern Alaska. Sitka lies on the outer coast and is some ninety miles south of Glacier Bay and ninety miles west of Juneau in the

Tongass National Forest, which is managed by the U.S. Forest Service. The Tongass is a temperate rainforest and the largest one left in North America. There are no wolves on most of the islands, and so we have a healthy herd of the small Sitka black tail deer, both on Baranof and all the nearby islands. Hunting season for bucks starts in August and for both sexes in the middle of September. The last day of the season for federal subsistence hunting ends the last day of January. Each man, woman and child is usually allowed six deer. Elders are allowed proxy hunters.

Hunting pressures, along with road kills, create orphan fawns, but often a fawn has just been temporarily separated when its mom goes off to feed. But people see the fawn and might not see the canny doe hiding in the brush. The fawns are adorable, seeming lost and in need. Kind hearted people seem to have an instinct to want to pick them up no matter how often they are told not to do it. There is something about the big eyes and wobbly legs that draws the casual hiker like a powerful tractor beam. Can a fawn live in the wild on its own? If it still has spots and is wobbly, probably not, for though we don't have wolves, there are domestic dogs who, despite the number of YouTube videos to the contrary, will chase down small deer and kill them as if their inner wolf had been awakened by a gigantic full moon. The most active deer killer I ever saw was a cute little pop-eyed cocker spaniel who lived out at a winter logging camp. He would run on top of the crusty spring snow and bring down adult deer by the dozens, only to rip out their throats, and then wiggle his way back to camp and try to cuddle with his mistress, blood red muzzle, paws and all.

What most good Samaritans don't realize is that one touch of a human's scent will cause a fawn to be rejected by other deer. It will not find a surrogate doe to suckle. It will not find the protection of a family unit. It will smell like a hunter to other deer and the other deer will flee. Most fawns left alone in the wild will die—killed by a dog, or a car, or a bear (we also have more brown bears on Baranof than in all the rest of North America).

So, good hearted people pick up the fawns. Sometimes they take them home, and they are cute for a day, but then there is the constant bottle feeding and the bleating, and the noise of them walking around on the hardwood floors, and the kids and the dogs are going to hurt them. So, they bring them to the veterinarian's office, and for many years this meant Burgess Bauder.

Burgess took fawns in. He always gave the well-intentioned people good information about deer, in the form of a loud lecture or a funny story told in an outrageous accent. The story for rescued deer rarely ends well. Small deer grow large. They become dependent on their human food source and return to it, but between feedings they'll wander, and when they do, they get killed. When deer are still very small, they'll get taken by eagles which also proliferate around here. (I once saw an eagle land in a tree with half a house cat in its talons.)

So, Burgess at first raised one fawn to the size of a Great Dane and knew it was coming into a greater risk. Another geography lesson… Sitka, Alaska…not farm land. Wild, but not rural really. Baranof is almost eighty miles long and perhaps fifteen miles wide at its widest. It has three small towns on it. The town of Baranof on the east side, Port Alexander on the south end, Sitka on the mid-northwest side. Sitka is by far the largest community with about 9,000 people and seventeen miles of main road. The other two have several dozen people at most and no roads to speak of.

So, Sitka is crowded in against the mountains and forest on one side and the ocean on the other. Forget the wide tundra valleys of the northern arctic regions you have seen in photos. It's steep-sided, thick with underbrush, and wooded. Houses are very close together. There are no roads in or out. There are too many cars because no one ships their cars off the island unless they go out as junk, which people are generally too cheap to do. So, it's too crowded to build a corral or some kind of enclosure for a pet deer. Even a local vet, if so inclined, just wouldn't do it. Even if you lived in west Texas you probably wouldn't do it. Deer need too much space, and they eventually will get out. Let's face it, as cute as they are, deer make heartbreaking pets because they end up running away or dead.

Now Burgess had this adorable animal who was about to run off or get killed by one of the local playful Labrador retrievers. He needed to find another island with a caretaker who could watch out for a feral deer.

Barry's island became the new home for the feral deer. Burgess brought them out so that Barry could watch over them. Barry cut the antlers off the bucks, and he sewed blaze-orange vests for all the deer so as to further dissuade hunters from shooting the animals from boats, which is illegal but happens nonetheless.

The deer were Barry's constant companions on the island out on the outer coast. The largest of the bucks would push open his cabin door and crawl up onto the couch with Barry and watch the small television with him when the football game was on in the evening and the generator hummed in the background. Barry and his deer would sometimes walk together on the beach at low tide, and the buck would nibble on the salty fronds of seaweed caught around the barnacle-encrusted rocks.

After Barry told me these stories, he smiled, with his eyes closed, remembering his times of happiness.

"I just love, the guy," he said, "I want you to write a book about him."

But still…I didn't want to. "What happens if Burgess doesn't want me to write a book about him?"

"I will take care of him."

"What if I can't sell it?"

"I don't care. I have decided on this. Have a few printed, sell what you can. I don't care."

"You don't care if this biography reads like a crime story?"

"No." Barry opened his eyes and paused for a while. "Listen, I know you write fiction. You can make some unimportant details up. You know, I get that storytelling is your business, but there are lots of good true stories about Burgess." Then Barry looked at his pizza for a moment and added: "Just don't have him commit any crimes," and he smiled at me weakly. "It will be easy. He is a hell of a guy."

Burgess Bauder *would* fit nicely in a crime novel. He is not huge, but he is battered, now in his seventies. He was the smallest lineman in what was called the PAC-8 back in 1963 when he started for the Washington State Cougars. He is a commercial fisheries diver to this day, and has racked up his share of near death experiences, diving for geoducks. Along with his intense intellect, his body still carries a certain kind of broken-down cowboy energy when he walks. For years he didn't cut his hair, and he had an unusual gait while stomping around town, a sort of windblown, elbows pumping strut, even on a calm day. Now he goes for the shaved-head, hard-time convict look. And he really is adorable holding a kitten. Truthfully, as a character, he is almost too good to be true.

Of course, now I had to make the decision on my own, whether to write about him or not. I thanked Barry for the pizza and went home to think about it.

I had never thought of loving Burgess Bauder. Burgess is loud and odd. He is the kind of man that gives the impression of being filled with a nervous energy that expresses itself in ridiculous fake accents. He has a Scottish doctor, and you can tell if he has seen him in the last month because his outrageous brogue never lets up. "Howwww Arrryaaa Ladddie." Also, in any kind of awkward situation where some intellectual capital may be at stake, Burgess needs to be the funniest, smartest, most outrageous man in the room. Of course, the problem is that I do too, and that can't happen when the vet is around.

Barry Burger had no doubts—he wanted me to write a glowing biography of Burgess Bauder, the Saint Francis of Sitka, Alaska. But Burgess isn't really a Saint Francis type. I can't imagine the monk as a defensive lineman in the PAC-8 or enjoying terrible ethnic impressions as much as our veterinarian enjoys them.

I went through my old journals and looked at what I had written in the past about Burgess. I found some notes on the time we took our old black Labrador named Otis in to be put down. Jan and I have only owned labs or lab mixes in the forty years we have lived in Sitka. Otis was an old swayback lab who liked to rest in front of the fire or on the steps of our house. Then Otis started teetering and falling over. He was old and we knew his time was coming. I called Burgess and he agreed to help us down at the clinic. Jan loved this old dog so much she broke down into tears, even though she wanted to be strong as she told our small son Finn that it was time to end our pet's suffering. We piled into the beat up station wagon and traveled to the shed that Burgess used as his office. While Jan and Finn waited in the car, crying, with Otis lying on their laps, I waited in line inside the old concrete clinic.

Ahead of me was an older man, holding an old Dachshund who had a grey muzzle and listless eyes and was taking short shallow breaths. The man wore a thin chain-store parka. The old dog had a tiny red collar and his owner held the narrow leash. They both looked exhausted. While we waited, laughter came out of the tiny clinic, the door remaining open. Cats and dogs rested in kennels opposite where we stood. The old dachshund could not lift his head to respond to the whimpering of the bulldog three feet away. The air smelled like bleach, dog food and musty animal breath.

"CATS ARE NOT NECESSARILY NARCISSISTIC," Burgess boomed in his normal joking voice. "LET'S JUST SAY THEY ARE 'ABNORMALLY SELF ASSURED.'" Burgess is also a big fan of implied "air quotes." A middle-aged woman walked out of the clinic smiling, with a grey, long haired, adult cat who appeared disinterested in the whole proceeding. There was no receptionist, there was no assistant, there was no money changing hands. The man carried his sick old dog into the clinic. I moved up in line, leaning against the concrete brick wall.

"COME ON IN, COME ON IN. WHAT ARE WE DOING?" Burgess spoke in his usual voice.

"He's not himself." The man sniffed as he spoke. "He...hardly eats or drinks, he doesn't want to go out." I heard the dog's nails hit the high wooden examination table that Burgess had built himself.

"Let me look," Burgess said gently. I could hear everything perfectly from the hall, even though Burgess was shaken from his loud performing voice. He was serious now, solicitous, of the man or of the dog, I could not be sure. "Oh...oh...your dog is quite sick."

"He was doing okay just a few days ago," the man's voice broke.

"His heart is compromised...it's barely working. Look..." Burgess said. "Open his mouth, look at the color of his gums. He is barely getting any oxygen...roll him over a bit...it's okay boy...it's okay...." Burgess was speaking to the dog in the most tender voice I had ever heard him use. "If he has the slightest stress. Any stress at all and he could..."

"Oh oh..." Burgess stopped speaking and the old man started to cry. I was out in the hallway, thinking about what had happened. The old dachshund had rolled over, taken one look at Burgess and died. Easiest euthanasia ever performed.

The old man walked out of the tiny clinic, pale, shaken, still holding the leash, and at the end of the leash was the tiny red circle of an empty collar. Burgess had assured him that he would give the old dog a free burial at sea, which is another benefit of Burgess's clinic services—because of his frequent trips out in his boat to serve his lighthouse bed and breakfast, he always has time to drop a body off into the water.

"JOHN, I'M NOT GOING TO PUT YOUR DOG DOWN TODAY. I JUST CAN'T DO IT. I'M SORRY."

"I understand. That's okay. Maybe you could just take a look at him?"

"YEAH, OF COURSE, BRING HIM IN. LET'S TAKE A LOOK AT OTIS."

I went out to the car where Jan and Finn were petting and crying over the old boy. I lifted him up and out of the back and carried him into the clinic. Burgess was a little shaken from apparently having killed a dog with his face, but he seemed eager to redeem himself.

He didn't speak or joke. He didn't lecture in a stream of consciousness differential diagnosis as he sometimes did. But he examined Otis, poking and prodding, moving a small light in front of each eye in turn. Finally he took a long scope and looked in each ear.

"I KNOW WHAT HE HAS. I HAVE HAD THIS. HE HASN'T HAD A SERIES OF STROKES, JOHN. OTIS HAS A FRICKING EAR INFEC-TION!"

Burgess smiled at me as if he were responsible for the ear infection itself.

"I HAD THIS A FEW YEARS AGO. NASTY STUFF. I WAS DIZZY AS THE DICKENS I'M TELLING YOU…WHOOO…I LOOKED LIKE A DRUNK STUMBLING OUT OF THE BAR, I'M TELLING YOU!"

He reached into his cabinet and pulled out a syringe and two vials of milky white medicine. "STEROIDS! ANTIBIOTICS!" He jabbed Otis with the needle and injected him with a massive dose of one. "BRING HIM BACK IN TWO DAYS. I BET DOLLARS TO DOUGH-NUTS, AS THE OLD FARMER SAYS, THAT OTIS STOPS FALLING DOWN."

Otis did in fact stop falling down and lived for two more years. I called up Barry Burger that night and I agreed to write a profile of Burgess, something about the length of what you might find in *The New Yorker*. Not that I have ever written anything for *The New Yorker*, but I had piled a bunch of them in my bathroom over the years. I would hire a book designer and would work with the photographer Barry had chosen. We would print a thousand copies, sell them locally, and I would give the proceeds to animal charities on the island. Barry agreed, and he mailed me a check to cover the costs.

Barry Burger died two weeks later.

Burgess Bauder has a keen and brilliant mind and he loves language. He loves thinking big thoughts and making jokes. He seems to love absurdity and he seems to always be in a hurry. Burgess builds good, stout structures in a hurry, but his finish carpentry, while whimsical, is not known for its tight fit and finish. "JOHN… I'M A GOOD FINISH CARPENTER…I'LL ADMIT I'M NOT THE BEST BUT…LET'S JUST SAY I'M MORE THAN ADEQUATE." I once saw a pile of foam crack-filler cans about three feet high at one of his job sites.

Burgess also has a romantic side to his blustery one. He likes to build lighthouses. He built one on what he calls an island which, when I was considering the exact same property some thirty-five years ago, I saw it more as a low tide extension of a neighboring island. But yet…he built a beautiful white lighthouse that he has rented out for years and transports his customers out to in his skiffs he lovingly calls the *"Death Barges."* Currently he is on *Death Barge* number four. Burgess drives a boat the way other skippers might drive a bumper car. The hulls, props and the skegs of the *Death Barges* are as battered as the hide of Moby Dick.

"I AM NOT CARELESS! NOT AT ALL. EVERYTHING I DO, FROM DIV-ING FOR GEODUCKS TO BUILDING A HOUSE, I DO WITH GREAT CARE. I AM NOT CARELESS, I AM JUST NATURALLY RECKLESS... AND THERE IS A BIG DIFFERENCE THERE."

I stood with Burgess once when he built a deck on a trailer some twenty feet in the air, by laying plywood on top of a lumber scaffolding and nailing it down with a pneumatic nail gun, then trimming off the deck-ing by walking around the edges running the tip of a chainsaw just ahead of his toes (safely tucked into his sneakers). Not carelessly...but recklessly.

People love Burgess, even otherwise meticulous people. It is important to remember this. Barry Burger had started his working life in Idaho, running a fastidious farm, raising sheep for their wool. Barry paid atten-tion to detail in all things; he could keep big equipment running by listening to the sound of the motor and doing regular maintenance religiously. He knew the importance of a thousandth of an inch. He was particular about the skills of the people who worked for him. He had managed several high-end restaurants in California and tired of managing people, so he came to live by himself off and on in Alaska. He did precise filigree carving for gun manufacturers. He could fix almost any mechanical system, but he was shy. His work, as a painter friend of mine says, "was beautiful and tight." He was the kind of man that loves Burgess, for Burgess does not appear shy nor does his work appear tight. While shy people are afraid of making mistakes, reckless people aren't, and when coupled with a fierce intelligence, they tend to learn things by leaps and bounds.

When they are not trying to get themselves killed.

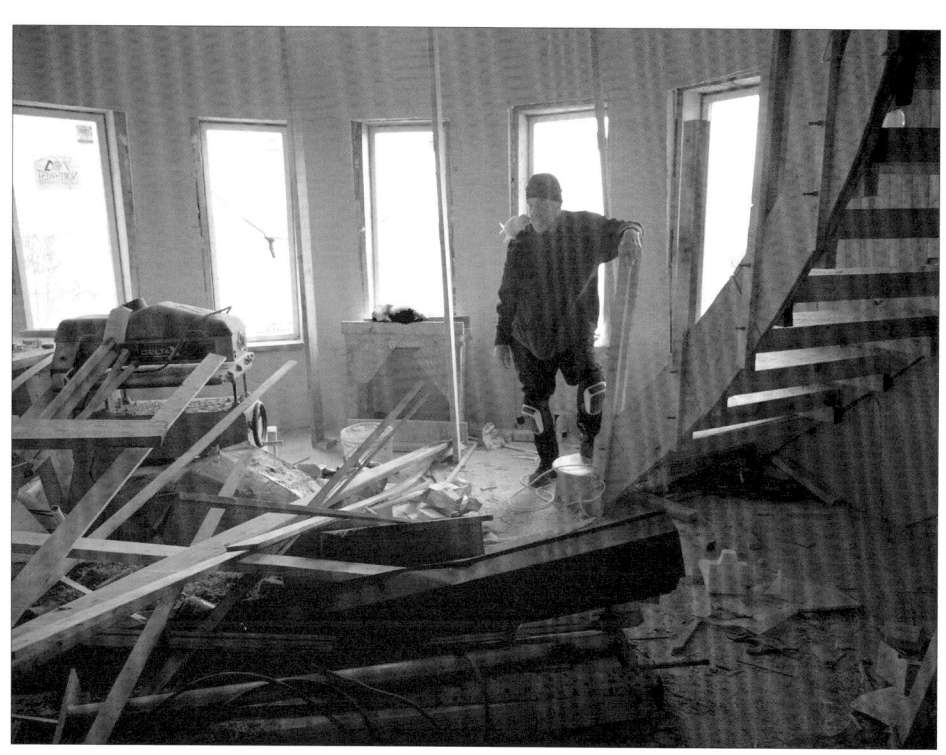

PART TWO
What's In A Name or a Place?

Burgess was born in Tacoma, Washington on December 27, 1944. His father had been born in Nebraska, and had bad eyesight, so didn't fight in the World War. He was a truck driver and a liquor salesman on Pacific Avenue, in the port city which had its fair share of drunks. Burgess recalls his father as being soft hearted and on a first name basis with all the drunks in town, who would regularly hit him up for cheap liquor. Some people in Sitka, Alaska have speculated that Burgess's eccentric behavior could be explained by drug or alcohol use in his past, but Burgess consistently and believably denies any need for artificial mood enhancement.

"NEVER NEEDED ANY HELP THAT WAY! I WAS ALWAYS FUNNY!" he would say. "THE WORLD IS RIDICULOUS ENOUGH WITHOUT DRUGS. JUST LOOK AT OUR PRESIDENT NOW. NOT THE CRAZIEST ACID FUELED TRIP OF ALL TIME COULD MAKE SOMETHING LIKE THAT UP."

Burgess is referring to Donald Trump. Burgess is a Democrat, though I don't remember seeing him at fundraisers or caucus meetings. His father was a Republican and he has a son who votes red. "IT MUST BE LIKE MALE PATTERN BALDNESS OR INSANITY. IT SKIPS A GENERATION!"

Burgess unconditionally loved his father even though he voted for Nixon. Burgess feels the same way about his own sons. He never discusses politics in the clinic unless something comes up and he simply shouts something out Tourette's style.

"OH THAT DUMB SON OF A BITCH!" he might blurt out and then go back to snipping off a testicle.

Burgess describes his childhood as fairly calm and free of trauma, besides the trauma of being an only child and having a funny name. "Birdseed" was a favorite nickname, but here again, sticking with a funny name seems to be a hard way he chose to take. His given name is Richard Burgess Bauder. But his father was Richard Orr Bauder. His father was known as Dick to everyone, including the drunks on Pioneer Avenue. Now the boy could have been Richard, or Dickie or R.B. or Arby, but the convention at the time was to be named after your father and the son was called "Junior," which Dick Bauder would not tolerate. "I won't stand to have a Junior in my family. No way," he is reported to have said. So our veterinarian is named Burgess, his paternal grandmother's maiden name.

His mother was Tyrolean and could speak Italian. His grandmother spoke the language from the home country but cursed in English. Burgess's mom was a lifelong Democrat and rooted for the poor and the underdog. She loved the old vaudeville comedians and the Jewish stand-up comics on TV. She herself was wildly funny and was known for doing all kinds of dialects and telling jokes. She worked as a nurse and loved her only child and took care of him tenderly.

Burgess explained to me that he is misunderstood in town. "PEOPLE THINK I'M THIS SUPER TOUGH MANLY GUY. I'M NOT. REALLY, I'M NOT. I NEED TO TELL YOU ABOUT THE TIME I CAME OUT OF THE CLOSET WHEN I WAS IN HIGH SCHOOL."

Then Burgess told me the story of his senior year in high school just before his birthday when his mother had asked him to deliver her

Christmas cookies all around town. Burgess had just gotten his driver's license and he was happy to do it. It was a long list of names and when he got to the "E's," he saw the "Epsteins." Mrs. Epstein was his German teacher. Burgess didn't want to go. The Epsteins had a daughter who had gotten into an Ivy League school, and Mr. Epstein taught the gifted, or advanced, students. Burgess was embarrassed. Besides, the Epsteins were Jewish and he was worried they might be offended if he showed up with Christmas cookies. "I SAID, 'MOM THEY'RE JEWISH! I MEAN WHAT IF THEY DON'T WANT CHRISTMAS COOKIES?'"

His mother brushed off his concerns. Everybody wants Christmas cookies. So he went.

Burgess was greeted by the four Epsteins and they all stared at each other. Burgess couldn't speak for a moment and finally blurted out that his mother had asked him to bring these Christmas cookies, almost yelling out "Christmas" at the top of his lungs or so it seemed to him. Mrs. Epstein took the cookies and asked him to sit down, and Burgess sat down and he began to freak out, thinking that they were going to ask him to eat, and he didn't know the rules of eating with observant Jews, and he worried that he was going to make a terrible mistake and was trying to remember what the rules were. When Mrs. Epstein came out with a class of milk, he remembered: "MILK! JESUS CHRIST THERE IS SOMETHING ABOUT MILK AND THEN I REMEMBER THEY CANT MIX MILK AND SOMETHING ELSE AND I JUST GET UP TO LEAVE. I SAY THANK YOU AND GOOD BYE AND I WALK OUT INTO THE HALL AND I FORGET WHERE THE FRONT DOOR IS AND I WALK THROUGH THE BIGGEST DOOR AND STRAIGHT INTO THEIR DAMN CLOSET."

So Burgess stood there. In the dark. He did not hear laughter. He did not hear a sound. Utter silence and he did not know what to do.

Time slows down in such situations…or perhaps it just lengthens out. "I WAS JUST STANDING THERE. I DON'T KNOW HOW LONG I WAS IN THERE. IT COULD HAVE BEEN HOURS FOR ALL I KNOW. I JUST KNOW WHEN I WALKED OUT THAT DOOR ALL FOUR OF THE EPSTEINS WERE ROLLING AROUND ON THE FLOOR LAUGH-ING THEIR ASSES OFF!"

Burgess had been a fat little kid. He said he had been 158 pounds in fourth grade, but he leaned down by high school. He started playing football in ninth grade and that started to change something in him. He insists that before that he was never tough or competitive. He claims he graduated high school with barely more than a three-point average. He spent most nights at home playing with his cats. Cats were his first pets and his first companions. He had a cat named Susie Bell before he was in kindergarten and she lived almost twenty years. He says that Susie Bell set him on his course in his career choice, for with each litter, little Bur-gess had to find new homes for the kittens, going from house to house begging neighbors to please, take a kitten. There was no animal shelter, and the tender-hearted boy who spent his nights playing with kitties could not imagine putting them in a burlap sack and dropping them off the ferry dock or into a river, which would have been a common solu-tion in Tacoma. When he asked his father why they couldn't get Susie Bell spayed, his father told him that the fifteen dollars for the procedure was more money than he had left over at the end of the month. Early on Burgess decided he was going to become a veterinarian.

When Burgess was in seventh grade, a pretty girl moved in a few houses down the block. Her name was Aleeta Wright. She lived next door to Burgess's friend John. Burgess would visit John and together they would spy on her. It took him more than a year to ask her out because she was "WAY OUT OF MY LEAGUE." Burgess consoled himself with his kittens, and with his English Bulldog. Burgess remembers that his childhood bulldog was named Fawn, but today Aleeta recalls that the bulldog was named "Mr. Troubles," and I have to say, I like imagining the young Burgess rolling around on the floor, telling the secret of his unrequited love for Aleeta to Mr. Troubles.

Burgess studied hard only when he was forced to. Someone told him he was bright, someone told him his IQ was tested at 135, and his teachers would accept no excuses. He made it into the college placement and gifted classes, but just barely. Burgess was a wise-ass to authority. A cheap laugh for his friends or teammates would pay off more valued dividends than the hard work and the smiling approval of Frau Epstein.

Burgess had some success as an athlete. He went to Wilson High School in Tacoma, along with the future infamous serial killer Ted Bundy. With Burgess as their starting center, Wilson made it to the Washington State High School championship game. They lost the game when Burgess snapped the ball over Butch Dunlop's head, preventing Butch from making the last-second, game-winning play.

Even after single handedly losing the state high school championship, Burgess was offered football scholarships to both the University of Puget Sound in Tacoma and Washington State University in Pullman. He was still set on becoming a veterinarian and Washington State had an outstanding program, so he set off to become a Cougar, at 195 pounds and almost 5'10" tall.

Football woke up some kind of fierceness in Burgess. Fierceness and self-effacing humor seemed to be his survival mechanisms. Pullman is in the flat country in eastern Washington on the Idaho border. The drinking age on the Idaho side is 18. On the Washington side, it's 21. Perfect location for a college town, and a good way to combat the bleak terrain and build school spirit. Still, Burgess had little energy left over for partying. He had to stretch himself to keep up with his required courses, and he was playing both ways on the freshman team. Starting line, offense and defense, every game. And he played every play.

In 1964, Burgess started as the right defensive tackle for Washington State. In true Burgess form, he listed his weight in the program as ".1 ton."

The Cougars had a new head coach named Bert Clark, who had played for Oklahoma on Bud Wilkinson's National Championship team of 1950. Bert was given the task of building a winning program. He was, by all accounts, nearly sadistic when it came to training. He winnowed the starting squad from 142 players down to 42, and still left standing was Burgess Bauder.

The defensive coordinator for the Cougars was a man named King Block (which could not be a more perfect name). One day Coach Block walked into the weight room and saw Burgess struggling to bench press 150 pounds. "Bauder," he said. "How in the hell do you stay on this team? Any one of these guys can lift at least half again as much as you can!" Burgess reports that after he finally got the weights back on the rack, he stood up straight and said to Coach Block, "WELL, COACH, MY PURPOSE OUT THERE IS NOT TO LIFT UP ANYONE, BUT TO KNOCK THEM ON THEIR ASSES." This got enough laughs to give the wise-ass another pass.

Burgess wasn't big and he wasn't strong, and he insists that he wasn't fast. So what was it that kept him on the starting team with one of the toughest coaches in the conference? Apparently Burgess just wouldn't back down, and he could move quickly off the line and quickly from side to side. His forty-yard dash was slow, but his reaction time was lighting fast in the openings off the line.

One of the first moves of the opposing linemen was to try and reach out and step on the hands of the defensive players across the line. Just at the snap, they would leap forward with their leading foot to kick the hand and bend the fingers back to the turf at the same time the defensive man would be reaching up to push or punch the blocker out of the way. Burgess and his friend Bill McCain would describe broken fingers and fingers skinned of hide, with nothing but tape to be applied. Their coach at that time would not allow them to wear pads on their hands, for fear of allowing the linemen to become soft.

Players who weighed 225 and stood 6'5" tall lined up across from Burgess, bearing down on him, and he would slither and punch them out of the way, occasionally standing them up, and rolling under and away to make the tackle. Each play was a fistfight, taking every last bit of strength and wise-ass underdog energy. Every snap was another chance to stick it to authority, and Burgess must have relished it because he never backed down. Washington State had never allowed students in the veterinary program on the football team. The thinking was that no one could keep up with the rigors of both, but they wanted him to play and so they allowed it. Burgess lettered all four years while he continued his studies and got his prerequisites to earn his degree in veterinary medicine. He was the only player to do this. He was also the first varsity athlete to complete a degree in veterinary medicine. Bill McCain remembers waking up at four in the morning and finding Burgess studying under the blankets with a flashlight. He asked Burgess what the hell he was doing, to which he replied, "I'M NOT HERE TO GET 'B's."

September through November the team practiced outside on those cold nights on the Palouse. Doing drills. *On your backs. On your knees. On your bellies. Push ups. On you backs. On your knees. On your bellies.* One night, the crust of ice broke under Burgess, and he sunk into the icy muck beneath. Finishing his push ups, he came up with a fat night crawler on his face mask. "HEY LOOK COACH! A BEAUTIFUL WORM! WHAT DO YOU WANT ME TO DO WITH IT?"

"Put it on your helmet Bauder. That will be the safest place for it."

And of course he did, and of course the worm stayed there for the rest of the practice.

Washington State had some rough years while Burgess played for them, but in 1965 they had a winning season. If you check on the Internet, they list Burgess Bauder as an offensive lineman, which according to Burgess is incorrect because he played defense. That year the Cougars played and won some close games against rugged opponents:

1	Sep 18, 1965	Sat	Washington State/Iowa	W	7-1
2	Sep 25, 1965	Sat	Washington State/Minnesota	W	14-13
3	Oct 2, 1965	Sat	Washington State/Idaho	L	13-17
4	Oct 9, 1965	Sat	Washington State/Villanova	W	24-14
5	Oct 16, 1965	Sat	Washington State/Arizona	W	21-3
6	Oct 23, 1965	Sat	Washington State/Indiana	W	8-7
7	Oct 30, 1965	Sat	Washington State/Oregon State	W	10-8
8	Nov 6, 1965	Sat	Washington State/Oregon	W	27-7
9	Nov 13, 1965	Sat	Washington State/Arizona State	L	6-7
10	Nov 20, 1965	Sat	Washington State/Washington	L	9-27

During the September 18 game, Burgess played across the line from University of Iowa's John Niland, a hulk of a player at 6'3" and 250 pounds. Niland went on to be a starting lineman for the Super Bowl-winning Dallas Cowboys. He was an eight-time selection to the starting team of the Pro Bowl. Impossibly, the Cougars won that game. How did Burgess compete against a player such as John Niland? Bill McCain, who played with Burgess that year, says that Burgess had amazing lateral speed and quickness, and besides, "He could endure pain like no one else I ever saw."

The hardest day for a football player who is 5'9" tall and 190 pounds is the last play of the last game of his last season. The Chicago Bears had sent him a scouting letter, but by this time Burgess was intent on becoming a pathologist in veterinary medicine. On November 19, 1966 in Seattle,

Washington State lost their final game to their in-state rivals, the University of Washington. Burgess walked off that field, tired and sweaty and beaten up. I imagine as he cooled down in the visiting locker room, it began to dawn on him that he would never again play the game that had awakened his deep passion to never back down. He would never strap on the pads and do battle in that way again. He would have to find another way.

Burgess claims he was never depressed in his entire life, but after his football career was over, he was twenty-two years old and had become "obsessed with the thought of death." He had three football friends who died in short succession: two in a car wreck and one by suicide. Burgess told me that he thought of death constantly for "about a month." He even wrote a note that he posted over his desk: "Dying isn't much of a price to pay for just having lived."

When I suggested that he may have been depressed about losing his football outlet, he dismissed it out of hand. "NO WAY. I WAS NOT DEPRESSED. I WAS HAVING AN EXISTENTIAL CRISIS. I WAS GLAD TO BE RID OF FOOTBALL."

From 1966 to 1970, Burgess finished his degree in veterinary medicine and he was looking forward to doing more graduate work in pathology. In August of 1967 he married Aleeta Wright, his sweetheart ever since the Mr. Troubles days. In 1970, three days after he graduated, their son Brock was born. Burgess was looking for a job and he found a job notice for a veterinarian in a clinic in Juneau, Alaska. He looked at the weather profile and it looked terrible--constant rain, bad winds, darkness and bitter temperatures—and he thought it sounded perfect. At that time he didn't want to practice veterinary medicine; he wanted to be an academic because he had focused his drive into his studies and he had become an A student and now he was a sought after commodity. So he decided he would work at the clinic for a while to get some money and then go get his Ph.D.

After several months working in Juneau, Burgess was offered a scholarship, a stipend, and a teaching assistant position at Texas A&M University in College Station, Texas. Being a football star was no small thing in College Station, and the fact that the Washington Cougars had been written up in *Sports Illustrated* years before as the "Cardiac Kids" for their close wins, and Burgess was an Academic All-American from that team, made him a demigod at first, but the climate and the culture in Texas did not suit him. He did not like wearing a tie, and much to the dismay of the Dean, he refused to pray at the required weekly meetings at his house. Burgess was expected to teach classes and the Dean did not approve of this wild temperamental young man from the northwest who refused to wear a tie and refused to pray.

"YOU GOT TO REMEMBER, I DON'T REALLY SIT STILL FOR PEOPLE SHOVING THEIR BELIEFS DOWN MY THROAT. PARTICULARLY AT AN INSTITUTION DEDICATED TO THE TEACHING OF SCIENCE. I WAS GOOD AT THE TEACHING AND GOOD AT EVERYTHING ELSE. I STILL AM! I JUST DON'T LIKE BEING TOLD WHAT TO THINK OR TO BELIEVE IN BY SOME OLD BASTARD!"

In 1971 in College Station, Aleeta gave birth to their second son, Beau. Burgess had a master's degree and had fulfilled almost all his course work for a Ph.D. in pathology, but by 1973, the Dean had asked him to leave before he had completed all the requirements. He came away from Texas, still a confirmed agnostic, and with a master's degree in pathology.

Burgess and his family moved to Sitka, Alaska based on a recommendation from his old boss in Juneau. In 1973, Sitka was a mill town with about 9,000 people. There were three shifts a day running at the Japanese-owned pulp mill. The US Forest Service had committed to getting 150 million board feet of timber to the mill, most of it meant for pulp used for chemical processes back in Japan. Some of the old-growth timber was canted and used for instrument wood, but very little. There was a small boat fishery for salmon, halibut and sablefish on the outer coast, and a purse seine fishery later in the season when the pink salmon started making their way back to the rivers. Tourism had yet to take off in a big way, and the large cruise ships had not started coming in numbers. Oil had been discovered on the North Slope and the Trans Alaska pipeline was being built from the Arctic Ocean to Valdez. The crab fisheries in the Aleutians were creating a new kind of gold rush up north, with stories of crewmen making untold fortunes in a few months of work. Alaska was booming and people were coming north for big jobs and adventure in 1973, but when Burgess and his family moved into their rental house, it was a drafty, damp, wood structure built on what anywhere else would be described as a swamp just off the beach. Burgess thought it was a perfect place to raise ducks.

Aleeta remembers that Burgess's dad had given them five dollars to buy lunch when they arrived in Sitka, but five dollars was not going to go far at the Harbor Café downtown, so the family shared one cheeseburger. A big Native man came into the café and slapped Burgess on the back and said, "Why, hello there Doc!" Aleeta didn't remember anyone talking to her. She had two babies. She had gotten her master's degree in teaching and physical education, and here she was with her football-hero husband on a rain-soaked island with no roads out. She said she cried for the first two weeks.

PART THREE

In the Fortress of the Bear

Burgess soon saw that Sitka was a rough town, far from what many considered "civilization." Materials and medicine were expensive. Everything considered modern conveniences were shipped up on a barge, taking ten days to two weeks. Jet service was just becoming established. Television programing was mailed up on tape and shown two weeks later than it was shown in the Lower Forty-eight. While mill workers had cash to pay for services, and they had the Mill PX where they could buy subsidized supplies, others in the community were cash strapped. In his first year in Sitka, Burgess put down an estimated 300 puppies and 300 kittens. No one had been spaying or neutering pets. Common and fixable animal health problems were rampant. Burgess decided that this was not going to continue. Not on his watch as the town veterinarian. He was going to provide service to everyone who needed it, whether or not they could pay for it.

He also fell in love with the place. He loved the wildlife, he loved the bigness, and he loved the toughness of it. He loved and respected the Native people. Eventually he even came to treat bears, eagles and ravens on the island, the most iconic animals of the Native community. Eventually, "The Fortress of the Bears" (taken from the Tlingit word Kootznoowoo) came into being. The Fortress is a nonprofit facility dedicated to rescuing "problem bears," and if they are young enough they might get sent to a zoo. Some bears stay indefinitely and are kept in an old clarifier tank at the closed-down pulp mill site, out the south end of the paved road. Fortress of the Bears was the brain child of an ex-Forest Service employee and bear guide, Les Kinnear. The Fortress has held on to four brown bears and several black bears. Burgess takes care of the bears' health needs, from blood work and reproductive neutering to the occasional dental procedures.

Bears, whales, and eagles are the big three charismatic wildlife attractions in southeastern Alaska. Our large ravens, too, bring a fair share of interest because they are numerous and they show so much intelligence. The Raven and the Eagle are the two totem animals of the Tlingit main *moieties* or basic societal divisions. A man born to an Eagle mother cannot marry a woman born to an Eagle mother, but must marry a Raven. Different clans are either Eagle or Raven. As you live with these birds you understand that they have power—observable power—in the world.

The Kiks.ádi are a powerful and large clan in Sitka, and their totem animal is the Frog. The story goes that they towed the frog with them when they first arrived at this place on the outside coast. From a western perspective, we have learned that frogs are powerful and important creatures because as amphibians, they are first to reflect the health of their worlds, their environments.

Another large clan in Sitka is the Kaagwaantan, and their totem animal is the Bear. Bear also is powerful for many reasons. Bear is obviously powerful to any person who ventures out in the woods. Deaths by brown bear attacks are extremely rare but not unheard of in our part of the world. The bear haunts many dreams, and it is wise to be wary of them when their fresh sign is visible when you hike. Native people all over the region have rituals and local wisdom on how to deal with bears. Most believe that they are not only sentient, but possess extraordinary powers to perceive. For example, traditional Athabascan people believe that bears can hear your words, and if you speak disrespectfully of them, it can bring you bad luck. Some go so far as to never say the word "bear" out loud, so as not to mistakenly cause offense. So, for instance, asking, "Have you seen any big animals around here?" rather than, "Have you seen any bears?" In much the same way that Orthodox Jews refrain from saying or writing the word or the name of their god. Tlingit people will talk to bears when they encounter one, calling them "Grandfather" and reassuring the bears that they are only poor human beings and mean them no harm, and are only interested in a small share of the bears' great bounty of food.

Burgess both is and is not suited for this mythological world-view of thinking about animals. He has a deep love for animals and a profound intelligence about them. He also has an understanding of the complex feelings that humans have for animals from his many years of experience. Yet his scientific training in the early 1960s was firmly rooted in a rather mechanistic western world-view. He was trained as a disciplined western scientist and, as such, he was told not to anthropomorphize animals and to be very hard and clinical. Animals, after all, were expected to be "put down," or euthanized, if they could not be cured. There were very few agonizing spiritual moments when dealing with animals. And yet, Burgess does agonize when animals suffer needlessly. He will go to extraordinary measures to keep some alive. He will also agonize when owners who could not afford veterinary medicine do not get needed treatment for their animals.

Sitka was famous for having many three-legged dogs, which surprisingly is not all that unusual for a small Alaskan town. Before he had access to his own x-ray technology and a more sophisticated operating room, Burgess had to perform surgical procedures in essentially field conditions, with the owners standing by helping. He saved many dogs simply out of deference to the owners it seemed. He once had a dog who had multiple severe fractures, on one front and one back leg on opposite sides, and he took both injured legs off. The two-legged dog recovered in the kennel in a matter of a week. The kennel door remained open, and on the seventh day Burgess came in and the hound took off running just fine, out the door of the clinic and across the snow. Burgess scrambled after the dog but could not catch up with it. The dog had no balance issues running on two legs, one front and one back, and only was caught when he jumped over a snow berm and became high centered and tilted to one side and was not able to gain purchase again. This, Burgess felt quite certain, was something the young dog was going to be able to adapt to, particularly as the weather improved, as long as he stayed out of the way of bears.

In his later years, Burgess had a lot of respect for the great bears of the north. But this was not always so. At the age of twenty-three he did something horrendously disrespectful to a bear and, by Native Alaskan standards, should have ruined his luck forever. He was working in Montana at a ranch. This was just after his football days, and he was muscled up and big. The foreman of the ranch used to tease that Burgess was "Big enough to hunt bear with a switch." One day Burgess was done with his chores and he was drinking a rare beer when a group of ranch dogs came running and barking towards the barn, and out in front of them was what Burgess estimated was a 150-pound black bear. The bear scrambled up a tree next to where Burgess was resting and the dogs barked at the base. At the time, Burgess had aspirations to become a wildlife veterinarian and he thought it might be interesting to examine the bear, so he went into the barn and brought out a stout lariat made of horse hair belonging to the ranch, and he shooed the dogs away and waited for the black bear to come down.

"YOU KNOW, BEARS HAVE TO JUST GRAB ONTO THE BARK OF A TREE UNLESS THEY CAN LAY OVER A BRANCH. THIS BEAR WAS IN

A HURRY AND DIDN'T HAVE TIME TO CHOOSE, HE WAS WINDED AND TIRED ALREADY AND HE WAS GETTING MORE TIRED JUST HOLDING ONTO THE TREE, SO IN A COUPLE OF HOURS HE STARTED COMING DOWN AND I FLIPPED A LOOP UP AROUND HIS NECK."

This of course begs the question, what next? Bears are incredibly well muscled even compared to the smallest lineman in the PAC-8. The bear tried to run toward Burgess and Burgess tried to run away from the bear without letting go of the lariat, which resulted in them both running around the tree. Once or twice, while the rope was long enough, they must have passed each other because, eventually, the bear ended up tied to the tree and Burgess was able to hog-tie its feet while staying away from the snapping jaws. Then he found a smaller rope and duct tape and secured the jaws, being careful to allow the bear to breathe. He unwound the bear from the tree and wrapped his feet a bit tighter and was able to put him into the back of the pickup and drive him to the main ranch house and corral to show Del, the ranch foreman.

Now in my imagination, I see Burgess covered in dirt and with a good many scratches on his arms, running up to the ranch house to tell Dell that he has actually roped a black bear and he has him down in his corral. In truth, the most serious injury suffered was that the bear had bitten the top of his sock off. But here he stood, the young, strong Burgess, happy and breathing hard, proud of himself. I imagine Dell looking up at him with a confused look on his face as he starts to get up from the table.

"How are you going to let him go?" are the first words Dell thought to say.

Burgess was crestfallen. He hadn't considered that.

They walked down to the corral where the bear was lying on its side, huffing. He wasn't struggling, but his hide was taught, and even covered in the dust, the muscles were massive and well defined against the wrapping of the ropes and tape.

"You're gonna have to cut him loose near that open gate," I imagine Del saying calmly. "I don't know how the hell you're gonna do it without getting bit all to shit."

Burgess ran to the shop near the ranch house and found a machete and a garbage can lid. He put on some gloves, and by using the lid as a shield, along with his 195 pounds of body on top of the 150 pounds of muscled ursine body, he cut away at the lariat and the tape, staying away from the claws and the head. Luckily, the yearling bear was probably more freaked out than angry, and once freed, he jumped up and rather than attacking the obviously crazy hairless being, he ran as fast as he could for the great wild woods where such strange beasts were few and far between.

It was then that Del asked the second question Burgess hadn't considered: "Kid, you know how much that lariat cost?"

"No" Burgess said softly, looking down at the horsehair twists cut up in the dust.

"Well, let's just say it cost more than you will make today and probably part of tomorrow. That there was a good one."

Maybe the cost of the lariat was all the karmic debt Burgess had to pay for fooling with the bear, but he had more opportunities to help big animals in his future and he would take full advantage of them.

The treatment of bears in captivity is a controversial subject. Many in our town do not think it is ethical to keep an animal, who in the wild requires hundreds of square miles of natural range, in an enclosure of less than five acres. Particularly if it is a re-purposed industrial tank, whose industry was responsible for the destruction of so much wild bear habitat. Some people feel it is cruel treatment of the animal to keep it caged. Les Kinnear, who runs the Fortress of the Bears, argues that each of these bears would have died in the wild. Their mothers were killed after getting into garbage, leaving behind tiny cubs who would have certainly been killed by hunters, cars or large male bears who attack and eat cubs if they wander into the big male's territory. Or, just as likely, they would have continued their mother's behavior and would have kept coming back to the same garbage cans until they, too, were shot, one at a time. Once their mother started getting into the garbage, her death was certain, and so too was the cubs'. The fault is the garbage can's owner. Les Kinnear argues, "Let's educate the people to store their garbage better. Let's use these bears to test better garbage cans. Let's save bears' lives and educate the people." Burgess and Les like each other because they both like the individual underdog, the animals whose lives need saving one at a time.

Once when doing a spaying procedure on a black bear at the Fortress, Burgess and two other vets had the eighty-pound black bear sleeping on a table. Estimating the correct amount of a tranquilizer weighs the safety of the human practitioner against the health of the patient, in this case the bear. For Burgess, the weight in this calculation went to the patient, and so he knew he had to work fast. Once opened up, the spaying of a bear is not particularly difficult. They were closing up with four stitches in when suddenly, without a moment of grogginess or yawny waking up behavior, like the scene in Pulp Fiction when Uma Thurman is hit with the needle in the heart, the black bear was up and off the table and huffing around the room. Doctors were scattering, instruments were clattering, aluminum tables were flying. Burgess tried to hold the bear by the back but was unable. The best they could do was corner her in the far side of the room, and Burgess fashioned a jab stick with a powerful dose of Ketamine and stuck the bear to make her go back to sleep. All the vets felt good that they had done the right thing for the bear by not hurting her and not over-medicating her. They did not brag. They did not disrespect the bear because they knew that nothing good would come of that, but they greatly tightened up their protocols and increased their dosage on the next spaying operation.

I have been attacked by both brown bears and black bears. I have shot a brown bear sow in self-defense as she charged me. I shot her when she was ten feet from me, her jaws snapping like an axe splitting hardwood. When I skinned her, her muscled body looked like a weight lifter's, or…a defensive lineman's. In North America, bears are the only other large omnivore that competes with the human for food. Bear is our dark shadow that hides in the forest. Bear is our brutal, hungry, sexual animal self. At least this is the role Bear plays in the ancient folklore of the sophisticated ancient storytellers of the northern climates. When Burgess played on the line, he must have been somehow in touch with some inner Bear spirit. How else to explain the fierceness with which he must have battled men so much bigger than himself? When he treats the small animals in his clinic, perhaps he is back in touch with Suzie Bell, his kitten. His current wife, Victoria, says he enjoys texting pictures to her of their cats snuggling together when she is at her work, just in the room downstairs.

 PART FOUR
Big Hearted

Burgess settled into life in Alaska. He discovered that he loved the island life. Some people from port towns like Tacoma come to love Alaska, possibly because those port cities were often the gateways to the north. It's possible that many of the drunks Burgess's dad gave booze to had fished for a time in Alaskan waters, or had cut trees in the old north woods, and or had dreamed of panning gold in the north. Many of the ships had come down from Alaska with hulls full of fish, in cans or slushed in ice. Some of the ships might have smelled tacky with pitch from the great fat cedars or spruce felled by the saws still roaring up the coast. The docks of Tacoma and Seattle were romantic with the promise of Alaskan wealth.

Whatever it was, Burgess liked the unforgiving nature of it. He started diving for crab and digging clams in the dark tide flats. He loved the coastal storms and the rain. He liked how the country was not meant for anyone of a mild temperament. Once, he hiked to the top of the mountain and filled his pack with a hundred pounds of venison, and on his way down broke his ankle. He still hiked the half mile downhill with his pack on his back on that broken ankle and counted it as a good day. He loved navigating his skiff through the dark and the white rush of waves over the rocks that passed by within inches of the hull. He loved the big animals in the tall grass of the estuaries and birds of prey taking the fish up in their talons. There was an electric energy in the air. He hated the times he had to leave Sitka, and didn't like going on vacations.

Aleeta eventually got a job teaching physical education while Burgess got the new clinic up and running. Soon enough she was the coach of the girls' volleyball team for Sitka High School. They were called "The Lady Wolves" even though there are no wolves on Baranof Island. The Wolves had two undefeated seasons with Aleeta as their coach, and they were written up in *USA Today*. Back then Sitka High played against the largest schools in the region, Ketchikan and Juneau Douglas High School, so their undefeated seasons were an amazing accomplishment for a little island town. Aleeta was justifiably proud and engaged in the community.

Burgess built his first building on the land next to the rental house and named it "The Hovel." Then he went to work on a bigger, finer house for his family. He kept the ponds and most of the trees. At their place, he cared for various dogs, cats, peacocks, peahens, cockatoos, parrots, and even had a rather large emu for a time. A few of the animals came to an uncertain or even a bad end. His emu met his when it got out of the enclosure and became entangled in a neighbor's clothesline. One of his yellow Labradors, who served as a daily walking companion, was killed by a brown bear on one of those walks. Burgess does not carry a gun on his walks, insisting that the gun is more dangerous close to town than the possibility of any bear. Once, his favorite cockatoo went missing. Burgess offered a no-questions-asked, $1,500 reward for the bird's return. They are certain the bird was stolen because two days after the bird went missing, the ten-pound bag of bird food was also gone from their living quarters. Burgess believes the bird was taken by a fisherman who somehow liked the exotic cockatoo and thought it would look good on a boat. "I JUST HOPE THE SON OF A BITCH HAS AN OLD WOODEN BOAT, BECAUSE THAT BIRD WILL TEAR IT APART STICK BY STICK."

I knew the cockatoo—she was an incredibly raucous creature and had an ear-piercing scream. I once watched her shriek and do somersaults around Burgess's shower curtain for most of a sit-down dinner at his house. I couldn't imagine living on a boat with it. I was betting the cockatoo was going to be returned after three weeks, but she never was.

Burgess taught animal anatomy and physiology at the college in Sitka. His students reported that he was an excellent lecturer: funny, smart, and well organized. They said the only problem was that some students found he spoke so quickly that they had trouble keeping notes, and that some were afraid to ask questions because he couldn't help making jokes and going off on long asides. Shy students at first were not sure if they were the butt of the jokes or not.

Once in a Sitka café coffee line, a man was talking about a problem he was having with his dog. His wife would not walk their dog because it made her queasy, and she would sometimes actually throw up because their dog would eat other dogs' excrement. He had said this in a low voice to a friend standing next to him in the coffee line and Burgess, who had, at that time, very acute hearing, overheard him and piped up, "COPROPHAGIA IN OLDER DOGS IS NOT UNCOMMON! IT'S NOTHING TO GET QUEASY ABOUT! IS IT A NERVOUS REACTION, SALT PROBLEM, OR A NUTRITION ISSUE? NO ONE KNOWS!" he bellowed out. "SOME DOGS EAT FECES, SOME DON'T." Then he stepped up to order his double-tall latte and a brownie, while the other patrons watched him and considered the truth of what he said.

These are the kind of statements that sometimes caused students to pause before asking questions in class.

Aleeta noticed that Burgess did not like coming to his sons' ball games. "You know, for all Burgess's football, he wasn't really all that athletic.

I mean, don't give him a ball. Burgess doesn't really care about games normal people play. I love him, I do, but he cared more about his clinic and his version of 'socialized veterinary medicine' than anything else." Living with Burgess was not always easy. He could not let anyone go without proper treatment for his or her animals, and he gave away medicine so cheaply that he lost more money than he took in. At first Aleeta would make up the difference with her salary. The boys enjoyed the wildness of their dad's adventures, but tired often of being over-shadowed by his…bigness…his need to dominate every situation and to be tougher and smarter than anyone else in the room.

Yet with animals and his customers, Burgess could not be more kind.

The most common reasons a person brings an animal to a vet are change in diet, change in poop or pee, change in sleep, change in energy, obvious pain, skin problems, ear problems, regular shots, travel papers, or traumatic injury. All of these symptoms could be indicative of a variety of problems that could be either minor or deadly, and it is the veterinarian's diagnostic skill that tries to determine just what the condition is and treat it effectively. Their pride in their work comes from the fact that they can do this without speaking the language of the patient, and by asking questions that can only be answered by body language, gentle pressure to parts of the body, the condition of the outer surface, and the demeanor of the expression, as well as a host of clinical tests that can be done.

For Burgess, the differential diagnosis for a dog usually starts with the phrase, "OKAY, GIVE ME A BUTT." The owner swings the dog around and Burgess puts the dog's butt between his knees, while the owner pets the dog's head and calms the animal. Burgess will often close his eyes and listen to the owner describe his or her reason for bringing the dog in.

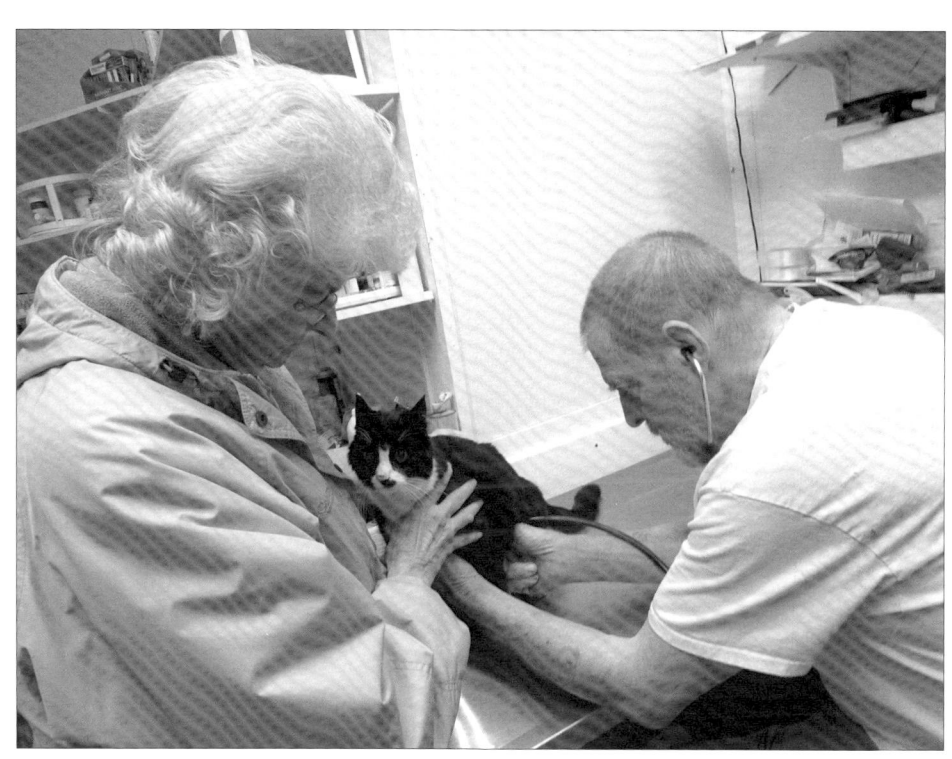

By this point we know it's not a traumatic accident. Burgess keeps his eyes shut and he asks questions that go along with a medical history: age, diet, how often the dog gets out, other pets in the environment, when was the last time the dog was seen and for what... Then Burgess opens his eyes and looks the dog over critically, touching almost every part of the body, gently probing. He speaks in a stream of consciousness, giving a basic lesson in pathology of this particular breed, giving specific problems and possibilities that might explain the symptoms. He doesn't bear down hard on these as answers, just as suggestions. He asks a few more questions. He will take some instruments and look in the ears, and depending on the complaint, look in the mouth and at the teeth. He will continue talking about the various possibilities, narrowing down the list to his favorite two. He then will shift to possible treatments, weaving in a discussion of costs. He will give each owner the option to pursue the expensive, possibly more invasive treatment, including the possibility of flying the pet down to Washington State in Pullman; this offer is genuine and Burgess offers to call the experts to set up a consultation, saying that they are great doctors and he knows them all and talks to them all the time, which is true.

Burgess goes on to describe another treatment, which usually involves the taking of a low-cost medication and careful monitoring by the owner for one day to one week to look for any signs of change. If they do not see the hoped-for change then they can either fly the animal out or take their pet to another vet in town. (Currently there are two other vets in Sitka.) He always gives the owner the option of choosing the higher priced procedure.

Most clients accept the low-cost option. Burgess either gives the pet a shot or he hands over a bottle with the prescribed amount of medication and the instructions written on the label. When the owner offers to pay, Burgess will name a price, almost always under ten dollars and wave them off, telling them gently, "Pay me when you come in and your dog is feeling better."

I have observed Burgess now with perhaps a hundred clients. I have seen money change hands maybe a dozen times. His office shelves have cans of smoked salmon and there are often cookies on plates. He stuffs cash in his pockets. He has a good accountant who does his taxes, and Burgess jokes that his accountant does his laundry too so as to get a precise number for his income.

I once spent about forty-five minutes with a Native man and his wife in Burgess's clinic. The man was old, and he had a very old dog who looked to be a terrier of some sort. The couple needed shots and travel papers so that the dog could travel because the man had to go to Seattle for health reasons. They spent a long time in the clinic. Burgess caressed the dog, checking for soreness and frailty. The dog loved it. Many dogs don't react to Burgess in that way, but this dog seemed to relish his touch. Burgess was concerned if the old dog was really up to this important trip. So they spent a long time talking, the owners and Burgess, the conversation more about comfort and relaxation, a relaxation of the anxiety of travel for both the owner and the old dog. Burgess took his time and everyone left feeling better about the trip, though no real diagnosis was made.

Not all Burgess-dog interactions go this way.

Once I knew a man who bought a Rottweiler puppy. He had had a Rottweiler as a child and it had been a favorite pet. He had bought this pup during the time of the puppy farms when Rots were popular. Burgess came by for a social visit and he looked at the dog, walking up to it and sniffing around for perhaps thirty seconds, and then he said, "YOU SHOULD HAVE ME PUT THAT PUP DOWN TOMORROW. HE'S WRONG, AND HE WILL NEVER BE RIGHT. TRUST ME, I'M RIGHT ABOUT THIS."

And he was, at least for my friend's family and the family that got him afterward. The dog would attack and want to kill other dogs and small children. Finally the dog was given to a professional trainer and was trained to accompany women who ran alone through dangerous neighborhoods at night, and then back to his kennel. He had to be kept on a short leash. Burgess said he could tell there was something wrong with the puppy by the way he cowered. "PUPPIES SHOULD COME TOWARDS YOU AND BE GOOFY AND SLOBBERY AND FUN. A PUPPY THAT COWERS AND GROWLS SHOULD GO TO A PROFESSIONAL TRAINER OR BE PUT DOWN."

Years ago, there was a rumor around town that Burgess Bauder wasn't a licensed or even graduated veterinarian because he didn't charge enough money. Burgess had his diplomas on the clinic walls, but some people thought they were fakes. Some even checked his credentials by phone. Others didn't care. Their pets got better with the medicine they'd received, and Burgess could be reached any time day or night.

Burgess has been called from bed in the middle of the night, walking across the street to his clinic to deal with weeping dog owners and doing what he can for their pets. Pet owners will stand under his window in the middle of the night, calling with their loud voices for him to come down and help. I took our old lab Otis in once when he snuck out on a dark, rainy night. I got a call from someone who told me that Otis was lying on the highway, and I said that it wasn't possible because he was "right here under the table," but when I looked, he wasn't. I found him on the road, obviously injured by a car, and with the help of my neighbor, I slid the old dog onto a sheet of plywood. While Jan called Burgess, interrupting his dinner, I drove Otis to the clinic. Burgess did not give me the scolding I deserved about letting our dog run loose at night. He patiently examined Otis and gave him pain medications and splinted his badly broken leg. He gave me an appointment for the next day when he pinned the old dog's leg and patched him up.

As the rain pours down on any of the owners coming in on those nights, Burgess always has a kind and soothing word for them.

"Gosh, I'm sorry Jan. Let's see what we can do for Otis," he said that night, as he helped us the last few feet into the clinic, covering Jan from the rain.

Otis never walked well after that accident but that was okay. He didn't wander far and that suited us fine. Burgess wasn't satisfied with the outcome, and he didn't charge us nearly what the work was worth. For years now, Jan puts money into Burgess's hardware store account without his knowing it. It's just easier that way.

PART FIVE
The Hard Things Are Never Easy

Once when Burgess felt it was time to take up in-line skating he started off with full force and abandon. Of course, he never begins anything half-heartedly, and he burned out the road with what I assumed was reckless but not careless speed. But when he fell he broke his hip. He lay on the ground until a passing motorist found him. Now by this time, Burgess suffered from many painful conditions—arthritis, ulcerative colitis, and an auto immune disease, which can cause his body to attack the soft tissue in his circulatory system. He had also lived through at least two other near death experiences. He is extremely tough, but he should be more kind to his body. The motorist took Burgess to the emergency room, where frankly he should have a card on file where he earns some kind of points toward a free hip replacement. The staff took care of the most emergent problems and then his friend, the Scottish Dr. Totten, came in, and Burgess asked him to fix his hip. This is how I imagine the conversation went:

Dr. Totten: "But Burgess, you know I am not really that kind of surgeon. You would be much better off going to Seattle where the doctors do hundreds of them a month."

Burgess: "Auck Laddie, Yew kneeew, Iyee would naught heve another doctor saw en me bones bet yewwww."

It must have gone on like this for a few minutes, with Burgess insisting in the worst possible brogue that Dr. Totten do the hip surgery. Finally Dr. Totten, after some consultation with family and friends and possibly an attorney, had Burgess sign perhaps the longest and strangest waiver

58

ever, and he did the hip operation and Burgess walked somewhat better than our dog Otis. But not much. But Burgess loves it, mostly for the story value, and for the chance to use his brogue and the chance to testify to the love of his friend the Scotsman who, I imagine, winces slightly whenever he sees Burgess's gait.

Burgess is notoriously stubborn about appearing to need help. Once, when he was building his current clinic, the one with the raindrop trim cascading down the side of the building, he was up on the third floor, framing out what would be the roof line, and he leaned over to balance himself on a rafter that was not nailed down. He fell some twelve or thirteen feet to what was going to be the second floor. He lay flat on his back. He opened his eyes. He was not sure if he had been unconscious or not, nor for how long if he had. He wiggled everything that could be wiggled and he assumed that nothing was broken, but whenever he tried to get up he started to vomit. He lay back down. He didn't call for help, because that's not something he does. But a neighbor had heard his hard fall land, then an ominous silence. The neighbor called Victoria, who rushed over but could not climb the rickety scaffolding Burgess had constructed to the roof. Vicky called Burgess's friend Larry.

Larry came right away and spoke to Burgess. The first thing Burgess said to Larry was "FOR GOD SAKE DON'T CALL THE DOCTORS. I'M FINE. JUST HELP ME GET DOWN." Larry tried to move him, watched him puke and refused. They discussed serious head injuries, and Vicky called 911, but she insisted that the EMTs not put the call out on the radio. The EMTs, who by now were intimately familiar with Burgess and his personality, understood and did not call out their run on the radio. When they arrived and examined the fallen veterinarian, they told him that they were going to have to put him on a back board, then put him in a basket and lower him off the building and get him to the ER.

Burgess refused to be put in the basket. "GUYS… JESUS CHRIST. I'M FINE. REALLY." No…they explained he had to be seen by the ER doc, his eyes were not responding the way they should, his blood pressure was low. He had a serious head injury. Still Burgess refused to be moved. Finally, the EMTs got on the radio, reporting their address and asking the ER doctor for advice.

Now, the ER doctor was at the hospital and it was a slow day. He was an old friend of Burgess's. He got in his car and drove down to the unfinished clinic, then climbed the rickety scaffolding. He did not examine Burgess but said, "GODDAMNIT BAUDER GET IN THE FUCKING BASKET AND LET THESE MEN DO THEIR JOBS. THE EMERGENCY ROOM IS UNATTENDED AND GOD FORBID SOME KID SWALLOWS SOME TOY AND SUFFOCATES WHILE I'M UP HERE DICKING AROUND WITH YOU," or words to that effect. I was not there. All I know was Burgess let them put him in the basket and was taken to the hospital where he stayed for at least a day while they ran tests for his concussion.

There was another time when Burgess and Bill McCain were hunting on top of the local volcano. They had hiked up the seven-mile trail and gotten some deer. Bill said when he got back, he weighed their packs and they each weighed 147 pounds. They hiked the steepest section down to a small three-sided shelter which had a floor and a stove. They took a rest. Burgess started writhing on the floor in agony. He knew he was passing a large kidney stone. Bill agreed to hike his pack down, then return for Burgess's pack, but he had told Burgess that when he returned from the second round trip, if Burgess still hadn't passed the stone, he was going to call for a Coast Guard Helicopter. Burgess started screaming at his companion, saying, "DON'T YOU DO THAT. DON'T YOU DO THAT! I WILL RUN OFF INTO THE WOODS. I SWEAR TO

GOD I WILL RUN AWAY. I SWEAR TO GOD I WILL BEFORE I LET THEM TAKE ME IN A HELICOPTER."

Bill didn't argue the point. By the time he had hiked the twenty-four miles or so, Burgess had passed the stone. When Bill asked him what it felt like Burgess said, "IT FELT LIKE PEEING OUT A BUICK RIVIERA BACKWARDS WITH THE DOORS OPEN," but he continued that he would have rather done that than have been helicoptered off the mountain by the Coast Guard.

What is it about a man who wants to give aid to people and animals in distress but doesn't want to accept aid? Is it just pride? I would be guilty of practicing the worst kind of armchair psychology to speculate on that.

But I have had experience with people who have felt justified in their recklessness. I have spent almost thirty years as a criminal defense investigator. In that job, I have worked for lawyers who represent people who end up in jail for lots of different reasons. As a result, I have had a lot of opportunity to contemplate the difference between carelessness and recklessness. Some of these meditations have involved Burgess in the factual layout. Burgess, as we have noted, is somewhat complex, or at least has several sides. When Susie Bell kept having kittens and he couldn't afford to spay her, Burgess decided not only to become a vet, but to provide his services at very low cost. Which does two things: one, it makes him beloved among a large number of good people in our community, and two, it attracts some people to his clinic who are only interested in where he keeps his drugs.

Early on, the canisters of nitrous oxide in Burgess's clinic were of the most interest to a particular group of thugs and they broke in a few times, but they aged out of their criminality and on to other illegal activities. The cops upped their patrols and things settled down. But lately, when young chemists began using all sorts of opioids and tranquilizers, some of them began enjoying the Ketamine, and the two veterinary clinics became targets again. Burgess suffered some losses.

I began hearing from people I knew in my business that there was someone offering $1,000 for the names of the burglars. This is a rare thing in our little town because few people spend that kind of money unless they are drug dealers themselves. Citizens on the up and up always use the police or a tip line and offer an actual reward system, but never go so Noir as to go directly to the underworld. But as it turned out, Burgess knows the underworld types from spaying their cats and dogs. He had asked a prominent drug provider in our town to snitch off the burglars to him and him alone. The snitch told him about when they were going to rob the clinic again.

Before he had a suspect's name, Burgess slept in the clinic with a baseball bat within arm's reach. One time the thieves actually cut the power to the clinic and the security system. The speculation is that they entered through a door Burgess had forgotten to lock, heard the veterinarian snoring, and beat-feet it out into the forest. Now, what he was planning to do to the burglars I can only imagine, but I shudder when I consider what could possibly lay in store for a skinny Ketamine user who has cut the wires to a building and brought their cheap burglary tools in his little sister's backpack, only to find the elderly version of the smallest defensive tackle ever to play in the trenches. If Burgess had planned to BEAT THE HELL OUT OF THE LITTLE SONS OF BITCHES with a baseball bat, could he have done that with enough practice and skill not to kill them? Would the dirt bags who had heard about the reward be trusted not to try and implicate Burgess in some murder for hire scheme? These are the things that keep me up at night when good people start to take things into their own hands. Lots and lots of reckless guys think they can navigate the risks and can't. Lots and lots of them complain about the unfairness of this to me on the phone from jail. But I have been told many, many times I worry too much. All I'm saying is that I'm glad that Burgess didn't catch the Ketamine burglars and the cops did. They did their time in jail. Burgess didn't have to. But again, I'm a worrier in a way that Burgess is not.

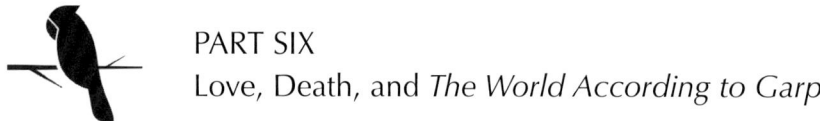

PART SIX

Love, Death, and *The World According to Garp*

Over time Aleeta and Burgess raised their sons, but Aleeta felt stifled in her marriage. She could not take the financial burden of supporting the animals of Sitka. They divorced. Aleeta still loves Burgess and bares him no ill will. When I asked her what she wanted people to know about Burgess, she said, "People should know that he really does have a good heart."

Changes came to Sitka too. The local pulp mill shut down in 1993. The town became a health care center for a local Native health consortium. Tourism and recreation became another leg of the economy. The Three and a Half Club, where a topless dancer once balanced quarters on her nipples, closed down, and a coffee shop opened in the back of the bookstore. Lattes became common and boilermakers for breakfast more rare. Where once there had been a bounty on bald eagles, there was now a raptor rehabilitation center, opened in a building on the hillside when the community college moved over to a larger facility, leaving a nice-sized campus for the center.

Burgess was part of the team that sought out the veterinarian for the Raptor Center once they had raised barely enough money for a position. He called Victoria Vosburg who had graduated from vet school in Fort Collins, Colorado in 1993. She had dated a man in Juneau and had worked in a pet shop in Juneau. Her boss at the pet shop gave Victoria a free reading by a psychic, and she went to the psychic to please her boss, not out of a particular belief in the occult. The psychic's name was Sayeah, and her name was in lights in the shop window. Victoria has said the psychic's shop was shockingly normal, but I like to imagine the atmosphere of low light and beaded curtains. Scarves over thrift store lamps. The psychic told Victoria that she would meet a man and fall in love. There would be animals in their lives, animals in cages. This man would not be rich. He would have an accent and he would be older than she was. He would find her a job and they would be married and they would be quite comfortable together. The psychic was certain they would be happy.

Victoria would remember the psychic's prediction because of its specificity. She met veterinarians in Juneau, and she took business courses in Colorado and wanted to come back to Alaska, and she investigated the possibility of starting a traveling veterinary practice, either on a boat or as a fly-in practice. She sent out survey forms to all the veterinarians in the region of southeastern Alaska, and the only one who gave positive feedback to the idea was Burgess Bauder. This was her first introduction to the Sitka vet.

Victoria remembered meeting Burgess and was struck immediately by his intelligence in veterinary medicine. "Terms came to him easily and he seemed to have an incredible memory for every case he ever worked on. He had a feeling for each case and each animal and each owner. That's what I remembered, that…and he was handsome," even though he was twenty-one years her senior. "He was also funny and he loved to do outrageous accents, which was the last piece of the psychic's prediction to fall into place."

Victoria came to Sitka and worked at the Raptor Center for $800 a month. Burgess had recommended her for the job to Dick Griffin who was doing the hiring, though it didn't hurt that Victoria was from Dick's hometown. Victoria withdrew her application to join the Peace

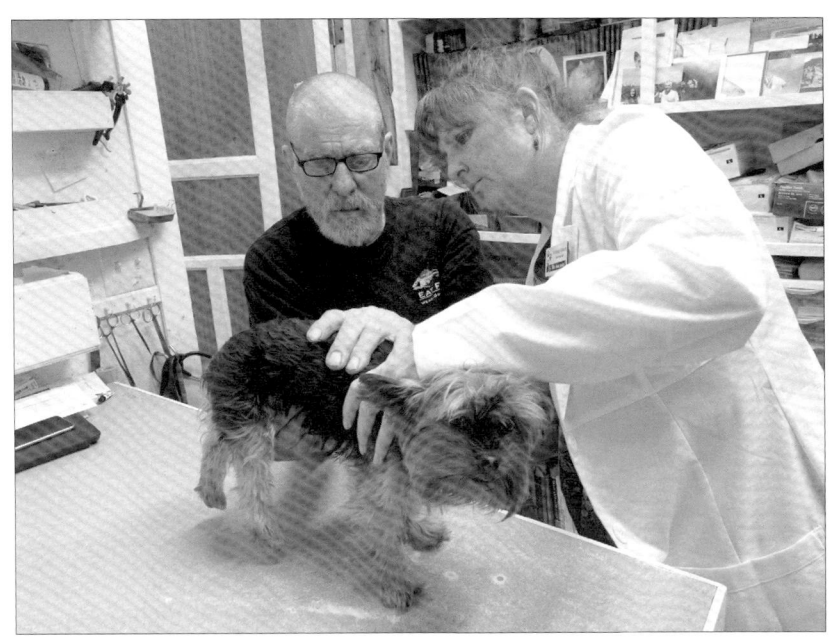

Corps and came to Sitka to tend to injured birds. Burgess found her a cheap place to live at the Native boarding school.

Eagles, owls, falcons, crows, ravens, all kinds of birds came to the center to be treated, and, whenever possible, released back into the wild. Birds suffer from all manner of injury—gunshot wounds; injuries from wing entanglements; and occasionally eagles will become electrocuted by landing on the two terminals of a municipal power transformer. Usually those injuries are fatal, but not always.

Burgess and Victoria shared collegial interests and social interaction, and they loved dogs and cats. They shared information on veterinary medicine, and Burgess admired her intelligence, work ethic, independence, courage—and of course her good looks did not escape his notice. Victoria has large inquisitive eyes and a sympathetic nature, yet she doesn't appear to take crap from anybody, and she speaks her mind.

They were married in 2003.

Eventually, Victoria's and Burgess's practices were housed in the same building, but not under the same business. Victoria insisted that Burgess keep his own books, keep track of his own records and his own costs. This eliminated the stress that Aleeta had felt with Burgess's form of socialized medicine. Burgess more than supports his veterinarian business with profits from his commercial diving for geoducks (pronounced and sometimes spelled *gooey duck*) and sea cucumbers in the fall and winter. Victoria insists that she gets a good deal of benefit from having Burgess in the office next door. "His knowledge is inexhaustible, not just in medicine and science, but in the individual animals and families of the owners. He knows so much about the history of the animals in this town. He has saved many lives." She admits, however, when he comes in to "assist" on a case or an operation, "he pretty much has to take the lead. That's just his nature and that doesn't bother me. He doesn't stifle me, and I always speak my mind when I have to, but when he comes in and there is an emergency, he is just off and running in the lead and there is no way to stop him doing that. It's fine."

There is no doubt that they have a loving relationship. If Burgess has two natures—the football player and the little boy who loved Mr. Troubles—in their private life, Victoria and Burgess share much of the quiet and sensitive side of the smootchie Mr. Troubles Burgess. They text cute pictures of their kitties back and forth to each other during the day, even though they are just across the street, and I've noticed that he mostly uses a soft voice when speaking with her. Burgess loves to share adorable stories of animals that have come into the clinic with her. Once, when Burgess had gone through one of his many recoveries from serious accidents, he was looking particularly rough—he hadn't cut his hair in months and he was walking like a stooped Frankenstein. Victoria was with my wife and they watched Burgess wobble across the road, and Victoria said to Jan, "Burgess is just so hot!" in a genuinely tender and passionate voice so that Jan dared not smile.

But there was a time after Aleeta, and before he married Victoria, that Burgess and the "Lovely Victoria" as he often refers to her, were living together. At this time, for some reason Burgess seemed bound and determined to die in an accident.

There was the roller blading incident in which he broke his hip, which he insisted be repaired by his Scottish doctor in town, principally because, I still believe, he liked doing the accent. But before that, he had been cross country skiing, and he fell, slid down the hill into a stump, and ruptured his spleen. After the accident, he still had to walk a long way to get help and a ride to take him to the doctor. This was quite a serious injury to have here in Sitka, and it took a great deal of persuasion to get him the proper treatment for this.

But perhaps his most dramatic near-death incident happened on January 6, 1996, when he was commercial geoduck diving off Larry Trani's boat with Larry's son Chad, near the island of Biorka, the same offshore island where Barry had cared for the rescued deer.

This kind of diving is done most commonly in Alaska with a hookah set up—a fuel-powered mechanical pump, on the deck of a relatively small, fast boat, pumps air into a tank that feeds air into a hose, and the hose is fed to a diver's mask or mouthpiece. The diver usually wears a dry suit, fins, weights, a buoyancy-compensator, a diver's watch, sometimes a depth-sounding device, and always a bail-out bottle of emergency air to breathe if something goes wrong with the surface air. There is also a hose called a whip attached to the diver's suit, which allows air into the dry suit to assist in emergency assents and to balance buoyancy.

When going after geoducks, the diver has a pipe attached to another hose for high-pressure water, and a bag for collecting the clams. When the diver sees a particular kind of hole or depression in the sand indicating a clam is underneath, he will get close, and use the high pressure water to blow the sand or sediment away from the tip of the neck of the clam. Then the diver quickly grabs the large neck of the geoduck with his left hand to capture it and place it in the bag on the left side of his suit.

Then he moves on to the next depression. Most divers wear fins; some walk along the bottom. Burgess had seen his friend, Spencer Severson, "walking" along the bottom without fins, working efficiently, and thought he might give it a try.

It is safer and more maneuverable for a diver to wear fins, particularly to make slow assents and to be more maneuverable with all the gear hanging off their suit. Fast assents can turn your body into a freshly-opened pop can, allowing the gasses in your bloodstream to "embolize" and bubble into your brain or your lungs, causing you all kinds of problems, which I'm going to call "the bends."

On this day, January 6, 1996, Burgess was not wearing fins. He was in a good spot and wanted to walk along the bottom in a hurry and gather as many clams as he could. He was some thirty-five feet underwater and had two clams in his bag when his shoulder-mounted weight belt, which was new and held together with a camlock, gave way. This weight belt carried some eighty pounds of weights plus his bail-out air bottle, and as it fell forward, it became entangled and held to him by his whip. Now he was facing down towards the bottom. He had no fins and could not swim. Without fins he could not right himself and get his belt straightened out. Burgess must have thought to go to the surface and re-do his weight belt and get back to work because he hit his whip and his suit filled with a bit of air, but as he rose his suit expanded and this caused him to rise more and more quickly. The buoyancy compensator rolled off his shoulder and it too became entangled and was fouled in the whip. Maybe when this happened Burgess lost his mouthpiece or perhaps he lost it at the surface when he attempted to call for help.

Burgess arrived at the surface still being held face down by his weights. He was drowning. He was about a hundred feet from the boat and when Larry first saw him appear, he seemed all right, as if he was resting on the surface. Larry heard Burgess yell "Pull me in!" and Larry and Chad began pulling at a normal speed as if nothing was wrong. But as Burgess came closer, Larry could see the gear hanging. He reached down and pulled Burgess up by the neck and knew immediately that something was terribly wrong. Burgess was pale and did not appear to be breathing. Larry reached down and untangled the whip, allowing the weights to sink to the bottom. He and Chad pulled Burgess up on the deck. Burgess was definitely not breathing. Larry began administering compressions, and then he switched to mouth-to-mouth resuscitation while Chad continued the compressions, trying to get a bunch of water out of his lungs. Burgess puked in Larry's face and then the Coast Guard helicopter was called. A good Samaritan from the dive fleet came to Larry's boat in a skiff and they loaded Burgess into it. Chad, and Spencer, who had come from another boat, took Burgess to a nearby beach where the chopper could make a safe landing. Burgess was soon in the hands of a flight crew and the Coast Guard EMT.

In the helicopter, Burgess apparently came in and out of consciousness. He remembers saying, "Where am I?" and then being out for a while. When he came to again he said, "This is a lot like being abducted by aliens," and then he was out for a while longer. At one point, when he thought they were getting closer to Juneau, he said, "This reminds me of the last line of *The World According to Garp*." (The last line of the novel is "In the world according to Garp, we are all terminal cases.")

The Coast Guard EMT noted all this down dutifully and gave his notes to the attending physician, which I think turned out to be a regrettable decision because by the time they rolled Burgess to the attending doctor, he was more or less back to his old self, and when the doctor leaned over him and yelled down at him as if he were a deaf geriatric, "MR. BAUDER YOU HAVE THE BENDS AND WE ARE GOING TO PUT

YOU INTO AN ATMOSPHERIC CHAMBER TO TAKE YOU DOWN TO THE PRESSURE YOU WERE SO THAT YOUR BLOOD DOESN'T CAUSE YOU ANY MORE DAMAGE," the first words out of Burgess's mouth were, "FUCK YOU. I'M NOT BENT. I HAVE NOT BEEN EMBOLIZED. I'M A DROWNING VICTIM. BESIDES, THE LAST TWO DIVERS THAT WENT INTO YOUR CHAMBER FUCKING DIED IN THAT THING."

So, the doctor certainly did not have an unresponsive patient. This guy was verbal. That didn't fit with being brain injured. But according to the EMT's notes, Burgess had been hallucinating. He had been talking about aliens and strange people named Garp. "CALL DOCTOR DAVID VASTOLA AT SEARHC MEDICAL IN SITKA," Burgess said. "I INSIST YOU CONSULT WITH MY PHYSICIAN, BEFORE YOU FUCKING KILL ME IN THAT CHAMBER."

The fact that Dr. Vastola was a pediatrician was not helping Burgess's case at that moment, but the attending doc did the right thing. Dave Vastola is of Italian heritage and is known as "Guido" to Burgess, who speaks to him, almost exclusively, in the most ridiculously offensive Italian accent. But like Barry, Guido "loves the guy."

The attending doc called Dr. Vastola for a consultation and described his mental condition. He described the comments on the helicopter, he described his combative nature, and Vastola said words to the effect of, "He's fine. That's his wit. He reads a lot and that comment on Garp was a literary quip. His brain is working fine. That's who he is. He doesn't like to be bossed around."

The doctors reached an accord. Burgess and a Coast Guardsman spent the night in the chamber, under a pressure that was agreed upon by

Burgess. They ate pizza and joked around and the next day, against all medical advice and after signing a raft of waivers, Burgess flew home to Sitka on Alaska Airlines. He kissed Guido on the lips, who, he insisted, was the second man besides Larry Trani whose lips had touched his own in the span of forty-eight hours, which Burgess felt was quite a growth experience for him, right up there in importance with dying.

Burgess marched over to the Coast Guard air station and met with the flight crew and told them that he was not the kind of person to write letters to the paper and fawn all over them, but he thanked them for their professionalism and their timeliness. He shook all their hands and let them know he was sincere in his gratitude. They gave him back his dry suit. Trani had gotten him out of the suit and then put him back in it to keep him warm while they were getting him up in the helicopter. The Coast Guard crew had cut it off of him. The suit was worth more than $2,000 and Burgess felt the loss of it dearly, but still he said nothing. He was alive. He had been brought back from the dead.

Larry quit diving with Burgess. Several of his friends have differing opinions of Burgess's distinction between carelessness and recklessness. Larry has said he can't go out with him anymore because he doesn't want to be there when Burgess dies.

 PART SEVEN
Choosing Well

Burgess built his practice by treating the animals of the poor and the animals of the people who like his brand of compassionate, participatory medicine.

Not long ago, when I was observing Burgess at the clinic, a couple came in with their dog, Molly, a red setter with large, liquid eyes and a white muzzle. The man was both blind and hard of hearing; his wife was deaf and had been treated with a surgical implant to allow her some useful hearing. Molly was a seeing-eye dog, which had been provided to the man by a charitable organization. She was close to twelve years old. The couple both adored Burgess, that much was clear, and Burgess and Molly seemed quite close. The couple and Molly were going on a trip and they needed Molly's papers updated, so Burgess gave her a thorough examination.

Burgess held Molly and stroked her. He talked gently to her and to the owner. Burgess's hands touched for painful reactions all over her body. Molly shivered and licked the vets hand, but never tried to pull away from him. Between murmurings to Molly, Burgess asked about how she had been doing. The man said sadly that she was getting old and tired. He kept one hand on Molly. It's hard to imagine a relationship like this—he not only loved Molly, but was dependent on her. The dog was getting old and was not as ready to respond, not as ready to walk as she once was. But her owner was loathe to give her up. Burgess gave her medicine to keep her free of pain as much as possible. It was expensive medicine, but Burgess absorbed almost half the cost. The wife continued to refer to Burgess as their "Angel," mouthing the words to me. "He's an AWESOME VET."

Two months later I was again in the clinic and the couple came in with a new dog. Molly had died. The owner was working well with this new setter, but the mention of Molly made him sad. He said that other owners in the Lower Forty-eight report that they have to spend as much as $18,000 a year on veterinary bills; much of that they can get support for, but some cannot. Burgess does not charge them for their frequent small visits, and only charges minimally if something substantial needs to be done. He charges very little for the medicine. The couple love Burgess and Burgess makes it possible for them to have a guide dog. Burgess said nothing as they talked to me. The wife hugged Burgess as they all walked out together. Burgess was clearly embarrassed.

The second patient that same evening arrived in a cardboard box. The owner was a young woman who wore a knit cap and had rosy cheeks. She immediately started talking about how "She felt heavier and her poop was looking good." From the box, up popped the prehistoric head of a chicken.

Burgess and the young woman engaged in a long, wide-ranging conversation about every diagnosis that this young woman had researched online which could possibly explain her chicken's apparent weight loss and lethargy. Her research appeared to be quite exhaustive, including a number of amateur chicken-rearing chat groups. Burgess listened to each possible condition and described its origins, often giving the Latin or Greek derivation of the word. Then he backtracked to the condition of her bird, to either rule out the diagnosis or to include it into the curative nature of the treatment. They discussed the specific chemical composition of the chicken poop. They discussed the shape of the poop. The young woman said she had read about botulism in ducks and wondered if her chicken could have gotten that from wild ducks, and Burgess mimed what a duck with botulism looked like, which I found amusing but the chicken owner did not. She simply said, "No… nothing like that." Then she asked about getting all six of her chickens wormed if that would help, and Burgess responded in his terrible Jewish accent, "Vorming es like Chicken Soup! Et couldn't hurt!" and he prepared for her a large syringe with a plastic straw-type opening filled with worming medicine and gave it to her. He told her to keep watch on her chicken. He told her she was doing a good job. He gave the chicken another shot of antibiotics. He said as long as the chicken is getting better you are doing well by this bird. "REMEMBER THE BEST PROGNOSTIC INDICATOR IS THAT YOUR PET IS STILL ALIVE," and the chicken owner thought this over and frowned. She clearly wanted to talk about it more, but someone else was waiting. She reached into her pack and gave Burgess some dandelion honey she had made herself. Then Burgess told a long story about someone who had made dandelion wine out of the greens and roots and the wine was bitter and horrible. The chicken woman was very sincere and assured him that the dandelion from which her honey had been made did NOT come from greens and roots and had NEVER been sprayed. Burgess thanked her and she took her chicken in a box out into the cold night.

The next customer had a tiny little dog that came from Ketchikan when the police found a house with a dead woman in it and forty-three inbred dogs in the house. The animal control officer sent eleven of the dogs to Sitka. All the males had one big testicle and one small one that never descended. "ONE BALL UP. ONE BALL DOWN. CLAS-SIC SIGN OF INBREEDING. THESE DOGS WERE A DISEASE-RIDDEN MESS. BUT THEY HAVE TURNED OUT TO BE THE SWEETEST LITTLE THINGS," and the little black terrier-looking creature with buggy eyes began licking Burgess's face.

Currently Burgess's life revolves around his practice, diving for clams and cucumbers, and his home above the clinic. Victoria and Burgess replaced the stolen cockatoo with a Goffin's cockatoo named Cora. A short list of their other current pets includes five cats—Fatty (aka Crisco), Drake, Gargoyle, Tucky and Stella. Two greyhounds—Ralphy and Lovebug. Several fish tanks full of frogs, gold fish and snails; and some unusual fish species. (Burgess is known to become upset when the aquatic snails spawn and release their seed and sperm because he cannot save and breed all the little snails. Some of the embryonic snails must be sacrificed for water clarity.) Vicky also has a cat who works downstairs in the clinic strictly as a mouser because of rodents who are attracted to the smell of the different kinds of animal food stored there. This employee cat is called Mr. Biz.

Burgess just spent about $40,000 on a new engine for one of the *Death Barges* for his commercial diving operation. He will dive with his hoo-kah rig all over southern and central southeastern Alaska in the late fall and early winter, often flying back and forth to where he has moored his boat for the short openings. Between times, he and Victoria will play with their cats in the apartment above the clinic that Burgess built across the road from his first house (the one he built for Aleeta and the family) and near his old clinic. Victoria and Burgess read books and scientific papers. Burgess is widely read and enjoys novels, history books, and keeping up with science and veterinary medicine. He is open about how much he loves home life. But he is also up front about what a good commercial diver he is and how much he depends on it to support his practice.

I asked Victoria about how she felt about Burgess's distinction between being careless and reckless. How she felt about him taking risks that he thought he could foresee. She said quickly, "That's him, and that's

80

the way he will always be. That's part of what makes him who he is," but then she paused. "But you know…I've been thinking a lot lately, as we've both been getting older. I love him so much, and I enjoy being with him. I just couldn't…bear it if he didn't come home one day. I really do want him to be more careful. Just for me…you know…because I love him."

Does Burgess understand this? I think he does, though he probably wouldn't admit it to me. As we age death visits us all, and for all his bluster, Burgess is not insensitive to loss. The loss of Barry Burger, the patron of this book, hit him hard. Often I will see Burgess in the store and apologize to him for not being around and for taking too long with his book, and he will correct me in his loud voice. "JESUS JOHN, IT'S NOT MY BOOK. YOU PROMISED BARRY. YOU ANSWER TO HIM. I THINK ABOUT HIM EVERY DAY. I DON'T WORRY ABOUT THE BOOK. THAT'S BARRY'S BOOK."

One of Burgess's best friends was the local magistrate, Bruce Horton, who was a joker, sportsman and a wit in league with Burgess. Bruce fell through his ceiling and hit his head on a new counter-top, dying in a freak accident that broke his family's heart and left Burgess without a comeback.

But here again Burgess is not unpracticed or insensitive to loss. He has died himself and come back to life, and he has also taught many people their first lessons in mortality.

When our old black dog finally was ready to go, Burgess came to the house. We had loaded the Otis into the car, but Burgess said there was no reason to make him uncomfortable, and he drove out to our house. Finn remembered the events of two years before, but didn't expect a reprieve this time. The old dog could not stand anymore, and for two days we had had to lift him to go out to pee. He moaned when we lifted him and was weak. It had been many months since he had chased a tennis ball. His eyes were hazy as if there were a glaze of ice already. I had dug a hole in the frosty ground on the point overlooking the water, as Otis rested on his favorite quilt. Finn and Jan sat stroking the old dog's ears and I waited for Burgess. When he came we shook hands, which is something we never do. Some formality of the occasion I suppose. Finn was probably nine years old. He was sniffling and a bit confused. Burgess sat with all of us on the tailgate of the old station wagon and he pet the old dog in silence. He gave him one last going over with his hands, touching him and feeling for the painful spots. He said softly to Finn, "Yes, it's time. See how much he hurts, Finn? See when I touch him there? That's the cancer. He's trying to make it stop hurting but he can't anymore, and there is no medicine and no operation that will make him better."

Then Burgess explained to all of us about the drugs he was going to give Otis. And what they would do. He showed Finn where the big artery was and how the drugs would travel to the brain and to the lungs and to the heart. How Otis would sleep, and though he might shudder and shake a few times, he would not feel the pain in his body after that. He would not feel the shaking. Burgess would make sure to give Otis enough medicine so that the old dog would not suffer. Then he filled the syringe with a milky liquid. He tapped Finn on the knee with his free hand, "You okay? Are you ready?" he asked. Finn sniffled and shook his head "yes." Then Burgess looked at Jan and me. "Everybody ready?" We both nodded, and he gave the injection.

Otis did not shudder and did not yip. Our best companion, who we had found under our old shed some thirteen years ago, took one long breath and was at rest. When we lifted our hands up from that good dog's body and wiped our tears, Burgess was gone. No money had changed hands. There were no platitudes and no philosophizing. No uncomfortable jokes. Just an honorable act of kindness.

While I was working on this profile I had an epiphany of an obvious sort. I was walking a ninety-three-year-old friend home to her room at the Pioneer Home. Her name is Nancy Ricketts. Her father was the famous "Doc" Ricketts, the biologist made famous in the John Steinbeck books. Nancy is a lively and well-read woman, a musician and archivist. She is as brilliant and as boundary-breaking as her father ever was. When she first moved in to the state-run retirement home, she became depressed. Depression is common with the institutionalized elderly, and it often shortens their lives dramatically—at least that is what I have seen. Living with the severely disabled, the stroke victims, and the demented can be frightening and disheartening. She and I were discussing depression after our walk and she told me, "I have a plan," and she gripped my arm more tightly. "I'm going to get to know, every single one of these people who live in that building. Every one. I'm going to find out what I have in common with each one. I'm going to find out the good things about each and every one," and she looked at me. "Don't you think that would be interesting? It might be hard with some of them, but all of them respond to something—music, sunlight, touch, warmth. They're animals after all. Just like you and me!"

Now, my epiphany was not about our commonality with animals, our animal nature. I had considered that long ago, probably long before I skinned my first bear. But what struck me walking with Nancy, who had been frightened and depressed at moving into the retirement home, was that people, even naturally good people, have to *choose* to do good things. They choose to do the right thing. Many people simply succumb to fear, and then anger and despair. Extraordinary people, at some point in their life, make a choice to do something good and they do it. Nancy to this day is getting to know everyone in the Home. She reads to people who cannot speak and she watches their expressions. She will choose a nice seat for them in the sun, and if they make a face at too much sun, she turns them to the shade and they laugh about the weather.

Barry Burger chose to commission a story about his friend Burgess who helped him raise Sitka black-tail fawns into tame deer who survived into adulthood. He chose that in the last days of his life because he "just loved the guy."

Burgess Bauder, after his childhood experience of trying to give away litters of kittens in Tacoma, chose to provide low-cost veterinarian health care to the low-income people of Sitka, Alaska. He chose to do a good thing even though he was a reckless, genius football star. He still provides that service to this day, as well as countless stories and terrible, accented jokes and observations.

As for me? Did I choose to write this profile? Possibly, but I still think of it as my own "smokes way," resisting and frittering about until I was finally overwhelmed by the good story Barry Burger started telling me two weeks before he died. I slithered past all the obstacles into writing a profile about an amazingly complex man that I came to love as well.

And the stories about Burgess are endless, and this profile is necessarily incomplete. Just as I was finishing it, I ran into a friend who asked me how it was coming along, and I told her I was closing in on the end and she said, "Has he showed you his arm, where he was bitten by an alligator?"

I said, "No...don't tell me about it."

"Oh," she said. "You should talk to him about it, it's good. I think it was an alligator. It could have been a crocodile. I think it happened to him when he was in school."

"No," I said. "Stop, this story has to end somewhere. I don't think I need a crocodile at this point."

"Or an alligator...It might have been an alligator."

"Or an alligator. I don't think I can use one of those either."

 ## ACKNOWLEDGMENTS

It turns out lots of people love Burgess Bauder. Enough to give their time to make a book. Of course, there were his friends and family whom I interviewed, and the pet owners who came into his clinic during the days I sat there watching, listening and talking. Thank you.

Special thanks of course go to Barry Burger, who got everything started and whose love and respect for life, friendship, and his community continues. I didn't know him, but I've grown to admire him through the friends he made in life.

Susan Royce did the transcription of my recordings, magnificently, I might add.

Liz McKenzie edited my manuscript, which badly needed it. She is a Queen and knows what I want to say when I don't.

Carolyn Servid designed the book, and her love of art, literature and books brings honor to this project. It was a happy day for all of us when she signed on.

And of course, Burgess performed the marriage of Ellen Frankenstein and Spencer Severson; they are both close friends. Barry Burger wanted Ellen to do the photographs for his book and he made the perfect choice. Spencer corrected my mistakes concerning the dive fishery from his long diving experience.

Steve Lawrie painted the portrait that appears on the cover. He is a treasure of our town, and we are inordinately proud of him.

Then of course to Burgess Bauder and Victoria Vosburg, who could not have been more kind or more open. I hope this book does you the honor Barry intended.

— John Straley

Thanks to Aleeta Bauder, Beau Bauder, Jan and Charlie Clarke, Clint Simic, and Victoria Vosburg for digging up photos from the past. We got many more photos than we could fit in the book, but it was time well spent with people who care for both Barry and Burgess. To see some of images we couldn't fit into the book, go to artchangeinc.org/animalnature

Thanks to Kari Lundgren for sharing her ode to Burgess with the "What Would Burgess Do" bumper stickers.

Our appreciation to Dana Drake at Panda Lab and Tina Miller at Harry's Custom Services for adding their touch to preparing the photos and images for the cover.

— Ellen Frankenstein